The
Natural Tucker
Bread Book

John Downes

Hyland House Melbourne

By the same author:

Natural Tucker
Natural Tucker Soy Source

First published in 1983 by
Hyland House Publishing Pty Limited
Hyland House
387-389 Clarendon Street
South Melbourne
Victoria 3205

Reprinted 1992, 1993, 1996

National Library of Australia
Cataloguing-in-publication data:
Downes, John, 1949-
    The natural tucker bread book.

    Includes index.
    ISBN 0 908090 61 7.

1. Bread. I. Title.

641.8'15

Illustrated by Linda Koukoulas
Typeset by Butler Graphics Pty Limited, Hawthorn, Victoria
Printed by Australian Print Group, Maryborough, Victoria

CONTENTS

PART TWO   RECIPES

ACKNOWLEDGEMENTS

My greatest debt is to my wife, Maar, whose encouragement, hard work and discrimination have really made this book possible. Apologies to Gerry with a broken back from typing. Thanks to all at home for their support. To Ray and Nola Murphy for letting me use their Buchan bakery. And to Anne Godden for her incisive editing and good humour.

Thanks, too, to Patrick Cook for permission to use the cartoon on page 13 which first appeared in the *National Times* of 24-30 June 1983 to accompany a letter of mine.

This book is dedicated to
my parents whose zest fcr
life has been a constant
inspiration to me.

INTRODUCTION

Bread is one of the basic foundations of life. History abounds with wit, rhetoric, rhymes, sayings and tales all related to the importance of bread in the life of man. Bread has always been symbolic of the 'lifeforce'. It was through bread that our ancestors could be sustained by their newly-discovered grain crops. They could cease wandering and establish ordered civilisations — based on bread. The bread of each society is certainly a reflection . . . of what? one wonders. Does the tasteless, colourless, prepackaged substance which is available today in our supermarkets and large-scale groceries reflect our understanding of, and relationship to, our food? It is certainly different from its ancestors.

Factory bread is bland. It engenders bland. Rather than being a taste itself, bread has become a convenient medium on which to array other flavours. Butter and its chemical substitutes, jam or other sugary pastes have become more significant to our modern palates than the deep and satisfying wheat flavour of real bread. What a thing to miss out on!

What is real bread? Classical authenticity results from using freshly ground flour, raising it on a leaven and baking in a wood-fired, preferably brick, oven. Today's real bread is home-baked with good quality flours and made with care. It excludes, of course, the additives and chemicals which have taken over the bakery trade.

Bread has broad nutritional, economic, ecological and cultural significance. The questions associated with it have implications far beyond cookbook chit-chat. In the nutritional sense, there is a great deal of controversy as to whether there is actually anything wrong with today's white factory bread. The scientific reports which abound on wheat and flour add to this controversy because they are confusing. Much of this results from vested interests who are only concerned with maintaining sales. They undermine the impartiality of investigations, by sponsoring chemists or researchers who produce the right results.

Apart from this, the variables in research are staggering. Wheat is grown in many places with different methods, and there is a wide variation in the nutritional content because of this. The methods of grinding and of preparing flour into bread vary; and this also affects the quality and quantity of the nutrients available to us. Our metabolisms also vary and, because of a host of other factors in our diets, absorb nutrients to varying degrees. It does seem, however, that a few trends are beginning to emerge, and that nutritionists engaged in honest research are starting to agree on some points. It is interesting to note that many of the principles of traditional dietary practice are being validated — in some ways, we may be re-inventing the wheel.

There is no doubt that bleached white flour is devoid of the nutrients contained in wholemeal flour. Even when bread made from bleached white flour is enriched to replace what are considered to be the most vital nutrients, there are other important substances which are not replaced. It is very short-sighted to believe that we are putting back all of the nutrients which are lost through refining, or to believe that those we substitute are the only significant ones. 'There are even subtler qualities or energy states of the protoplasmic constituents that our technology is not yet sophisticated enough to pick up.'* Food which is artificially separated and de-natured cannot be wholesome. This is perhaps the first area of broad agreement between those who are engaged in ongoing, honest research.

Secondly, there is evidence to suggest that wholemeal bread is not as ideal as some would like to believe. There is also research that indicates that bran-enriched products are even less nutritious because the phytic acid found in bran interferes with the absorption of minerals. This evidence is, typically, not universally applicable. Some people have no problems absorbing nutrients from wholemeal, whereas others cannot cope with it. Further, it seems that people develop an ability to absorb the required minerals from wholemeal after a period of transition in diet.

The bran which may cause problems is the very exterior of the wheat berry, not all of the bran. If this is removed, a flour of 90 to 95 per cent extraction results, which may be the ideal flour to use, nutritionally speaking. It is probably the best for children. A further complicating factor with regard to bran and wholemeal lies in the method of bread manufacture. It seems that when bread is made on the sourdough or leaven system from 100 per cent wholemeal flour, without artificial chemical additives, the complex fermentation involved alters the compounds which would otherwise interfere with mineral absorption and enables the smooth assimilation of the grain's mineral content. This is probably also true of yeast bread produced with a lengthy fermentation (at least four hours). Since it undergoes no fermentation, unleavened bread is traditionally made with lightly sifted wholemeal to make it more digestible. In India, chapatti (flat bread) made with Atta flour, has been consumed for thousands of years.

The third broad area of agreement is that the fewer artificial chemicals there are in the diet, the better. This certainly indicts modern white bread, which is subjected to chemical treatment from the growth of the wheat, through bleaching, to the addition of colouring agents, refined salt, mould inhibitors and preservatives. Some are reluctant to accept this point because the evidence is not absolute. We are discovering daily the carcinogenic and dysfunctional aspects of many chemicals, some of which were assumed to be harmless for years. The use of artificial chemicals in food correlates strongly with the rise of twentieth century-type diseases in twentieth century proportions. So does the use of refined flour and most other highly refined and de-natured foods.

That breads made in the traditional way have better flavour and aroma is pretty well accepted universally. The superior texture is apparent also, unlike factory bread which becomes an indigestible wad, if properly chewed. From these viewpoints, authentic breads have culinary distinction. You are really missing out on a satisfying pleasure if you have never made or eaten such bread. It contributes to a feeling of well-being if food with wholesome flavours is experienced — one aspect of diet which is often overlooked. A desire to experience authentic or real flavours indicates a healthy appetite, as opposed to a pathological appetite which craves unhealthy amounts of highly refined foods.

It is merely conjecture that the national health bill would be reduced considerably if bleached refined flour was not mixed with chemicals to create our staple, factory-produced white bread. It is, however, a conjecture shared by a growing number, and one which was mentioned in the US Government's controversial Dietary Goals. Because such an idea cannot be supported by objective scientific evidence yet, it is unacceptable to many. It seems the healthful results of eliminating refined foods from one's diet is experiential and, as such, not readily accepted by those who have not experienced them. The experience is communicable, however, and it is gaining wide acceptance in the community.

The issue of whether today's white bread is suitable for human consumption or not is also clouded by the fact that most of the so-called 'wholemeal' breads on sale today are no better. As discussed in the text (page 26), they are usually made from dyed white dough, with some bran thrown in for good measure, or are artificially inflated by the use of gluten flour. Very few scientists have used authentic bread in their researches. Those who do, report that real bread reacts quite differently from commercial wholemeals, which actually show little difference to factory white bread. Therefore, much of the research on wholemeal v. white has little validity.

More food value is available to us from real bread, and the waste of nutrients in milling required to produce factory bread is irresponsible. The milling process itself is a waste of energy. It is unnecessary to sift flour so finely, usually to 72 per cent, and the bleaching processes are an excessive waste of energy and technology. The whole process requires expensive machinery and so has allowed monopolies to gain control of the industry. The result is a de-natured product for us. Again, it is extraordinary that such foods are forced upon the public so that the monopolies can thrive.

Nutritionally and ecologically, authentic bread is at its best when eaten with a portion of dried beans or peas (legumes). This combination provides all of the eight essential amino acids needed to form a complete protein, the equivalent at least of meat and dairy products. The combination is significant because growing grains and legumes as a protein source is far more efficient than farming animals. One acre of land can produce fifteen times more protein under food crops than from animal husbandry[‡].

There is also considerable evidence that cereal grains and dried beans and peas are a healthier source of protein than animal products. It is certainly traditional practice the world round to obtain protein requirements from these vegetable sources, using meat and dairy products more as supplements. There are variations from this general practice, of course, but these have all been dictated by environment.

Asian peoples combine tofu or dow foo or bean curd, which is produced from soya beans, with rice, wheat, millet and barley. European peoples used wheat, rye, barley and oats, combined with dried beans and peas. In Africa and America, grains and legumes were similarly combined. Traditional cuisines, which have survived even partially intact, bear witness to this. As the US Government's Dietary Goals statement indicates, it is not that meat and dairy products should be eliminated from the diet, but that optimum health would result if they were considerably reduced — in fact eaten in the proportions of our time honoured fare, with variations dictated by environment and circumstance.

We may be at an important crossroad in our dietary history. The last one hundred years in particular have been characterised by dramatic changes in our eating habits. Many are now wondering whether these changes are the result of a romance with the new, or of something more sinister which may be inherent in our economic system. Do these changes need to be re-evaluated? The highest quality food is certainly available, but we reject it in favour of 'party fare'. Seen in this light, authentic bread is an important food having broad implications for the individual and for society. It is a medium through which to experience the essence of our civilisation. Baking it at home is currently your only choice. Besides being a rewarding pastime, you are creating a valuable food which bestows numerous blessings. As a cornerstone of many cultures, it is as worthwhile of restoration as those other aspects of our past we are learning to treasure.

Diet and Nutrition: a holistic approach by Rudolph Ballentine (Himalayan International Institute, Pennsylvania, USA).
‡*Diet for a Small Planet* by Frances Moore Lappe (Ballantine Books, New York).

14

ECONOMICS AND THE BAKING TRADE

The economic implications of bread are still with us, as they have been throughout history. Today, there is a different slant. Historically, millers and bakers were regarded as rogues, out to deceive the public at every opportunity. This was because some of them used injurious ingredients in their bread in order to increase their profits, ingredients ranging from alum to bone meal. Well, nothing has changed on this front, but today, the 'bakers' are huge combines whose aim is to produce the most bread at the least expense and sell it for the maximum price. This necessitates employing fewer bakers and more machinery, and stretching the law to the limit with regard to additives designed to allow them to use more water in the dough, with less flour.

Until the 1950s most areas of Australia still had their local baker, even though there were also large baking concerns. Granted, these local bakers did not produce additive-free bread, but it did have character. The 1950s saw the demise of the small baker. Bakeries were bought up by the bakery combines or flour millers and the neighbourhood bakery virtually disappeared. It could not compete with factory prices or with the web of distribution which placed packaged bread in the supermarkets. This is monopoly capitalism, to use a convenient but unpopular label, and it is the type of act which has exploited the public by creating less jobs and inferior food.

It is a pity that commercial bakers believe they have to use chemical additives and gluten flour in their bread. Some, of course, are aware that such ingredients allow them to add more water to the dough, thus producing more bread for less flour. Others seem to think that bread can't be made with water, flour, yeast and salt. The manuals sent out to bakers from the flour millers don't help at all. These provide recipes full of ingredients such as syrups, malt compounds, glycerine, bread 'improvers', chemical shortenings, etc., marketed, of course, by that particular milling concern or an associated company. An unfortunate side effect of monopoly mechanisation in the bakery trade is that it has brought about the demise of another human skill, replaced by the dreaded machine. Bakers have become food technicians instead of craftsmen.

By reviving the baker and the bakery, we would have more jobs and better quality food. This solution would be not a return to the past, but a step into the future. A case can surely be made for the scaling down of mass bread processing. I am not suggesting a return to the arduous life of the old-style baker, rather of using the benefits of technology alongside the wisdom of experience. This is essential if we are to have access to wholesome bread, which would seem to be something we all naturally want. An enlightened commercial process could be developed which would be easier than the traditonal hand method, and the bread produced would be of higher quality than we have today. Regional bakers would have a place and we would all benefit from the diversity of breads, as we do generally from a diversity of other products made by artists and artisans. This solution could be an economic reality because the public today is showing an increasing awareness of the value of good bread and is prepared to pay for it.

I know of only two bakeries/cake shops in Australia which are producing truly natural and traditional breads and pastries. The Feedwell Café, 95 Greville Street, Prahran, Melbourne, is not so much a bakery as a natural foods patisserie. It serves a range of creative savouries, salads, pastries, cakes and desserts which are based on modern and traditional wholesome cooking principles. No cane sugar and few dairy products are used. The ingredients in all foods are of the highest quality. Apart from this, the food looks and tastes terrific.

The Demeter Bakery, 65 Derwent Street, Glebe, Sydney, produces high quality breads made from freshly milled biodynamic and organic wheats. To my knowledge, it produces the only commercial natural leaven breads in Australia. The bread is baked in a gas-fired brick oven which has been converted from wood. The bakery is charming and very clean. Wheat is stored in a silo into which is pumped carbon dioxide. This allows freedom from insect infestation without the use of potentially harmful chemicals. Apart from the paradoxical use of refined cane sugar in their pastries, Demeter products are of high quality.

PART ONE

BAKING BREAD

JUST FLOUR

Most of us are unaware that there are different kinds of flour. 'My bread is a flop and I followed the directions perfectly!' But the recipe just specified 'flour'. The term flour is used in so many different ways that it is no wonder confusion and frustration exist with any recipe involving it, particularly for bread. Worse than this, in Australia flour is rarely labelled as being suitable for bread or pastry (or whatever). Even more confusing, flour is often blended so that it is supposedly suitable for everything.

The confusion arises from the type of wheat used by the mill. Generally, flour that is most suitable for bread is ground from higher protein or hard wheat. This flour is often called strong flour and does not make good pastry or biscuits, as the products turn out far too firm. Flour which is most suitable for cakes, biscuits and pastry is grown from lower protein or soft wheat.

This does not mean that soft wheat cannot be used for making bread; in fact, if properly handled, it makes superb bread. Although it rises less and stales faster, the aroma, flavour and texture are delightful. Generally, hard flour is suitable for long fermentation (4 to 12 hours) and strong kneading. Soft flours are kneaded less and are more suitable in short term doughs (up to 4 hours). Bread made authentically from fresh flour and baked on the stones of a wood-fired oven can be excellent, even though it is made with flour ground from soft wheat. On the other hand, the worst of the modern, high-rise white breads pumped out of a factory, is made from hard wheat.

However, the home baker will usually have more success with bread flour ground from hard wheat, than with flour ground from soft wheat. The higher gluten content of hard wheat ensures a more even and lasting rise. Soft wheat flour, containing less gluten, is more prone to flopping if improperly handled and does not give a good rise except in the hands of an experienced cook or baker. Most of us want a good rise so strong bread flour will give confidence.

But what is gluten? A much bandied-about term in bread baking circles, gluten is the protein in wheat, which, when agitated with water (as in kneading) forms an elastic strand which is clearly identifiable in dough. As the yeast or leaven respires, releasing gases into the bread dough, small elastic gluten envelopes are formed. As more gases are released, these envelopes expand and the bread rises. If a flour with low gluten is used, as the bread rises these envelopes can collapse at the final stage instead of holding firm, hence making heavy as opposed to well-risen bread. However, if you have only soft wheat flour available, you can add gluten flour to it until you have the experience to make acceptable bread from soft wheat flour alone. Hard wheat, i.e. high gluten, high protein flour, ensures the best rise with the least experience and good and thorough kneading will produce adequate gluten formation.

I do not recommend adding gluten flour to bread and I consider that bread made with the addition of gluten is cosmetic. It is also a cover up for poor technique. Further, I suspect that the addition of it to breads may be a root cause of gluten allergy. Some modern bread is made with a large percentage of gluten flour. One firm in Melbourne markets a wide variety of loaves — oat, rye, barley, etc — which are all of a uniform texture. If compressed, they spring back to their original shape as though made of an elastic substance. They are . . . gluten. This is tantamount to dishonesty. The loaves have no resemblance to authentic breads containing wheat and the other grain flours mentioned. The flavour and texture are empty, the loaves have no bloom and the crust is more like a skin.

Flour Availability

The following flours are generally available in the cities and larger rural centres of Australia. If you live in an outlying area, flour can be ordered from distributors in the cities. There are other types of flour which I have not mentioned or used. You can test their suitability by buying the flours recommended in this book and comparing. Judge if they have the qualities of the flours mentioned here, and use accordingly. Some of the terms used in this book are not familiar to the proprietors of many stores, or even distributors. Asking for hard wheat or strong flour often causes confusion. You need to be somewhat of a sleuth and discover for yourself. It's worth it. A good idea is to ask simply for bread flour. Some stores will give you what they've got regardless . . . so you'll find out the hard way. Often the best bread flour is not organic, which, depending on your beliefs, may exclude it.

Lowan Wholefoods, available throughout Australia, have the best range of flour and their cereals are generally organically grown.

Eighty per cent Cake Flour   Lowans are the only firm to actually label a packet Cake Flour. This is a great advance! It is a soft flour, milled from soft wheat of 80 per cent extraction and suitable for all non-bread purposes. It will make a terrific loaf in the right hands, but is not generally suitable for bread. Occasionally, a batch of this flour is milled from a harder wheat and is quite suitable for bread. This is obvious because it feels 'sandy', quite different from its usually soft, almost talc-like texture. Such soft flour is often called biscuit flour in Australia.

Lowans Wholemeal is milled from soft wheat or a mixture which contains more soft than hard wheats. It is generally unsuitable for bread, unless mixed with gluten flour or an unbleached white flour. It will produce a low rise, moist and somewhat crumbly bread, but is excellent for wholemeal cakes and pastry.

Lowans L.S. Wholemeal is for bread baking. It is 100 per cent wholemeal, organically grown and milled from medium-hard wheat. It is far better for bread baking than the above mentioned wholemeal. Unfortunately, it is only available in 67 kilo sacks. Perhaps you could ask a local shopkeeper to order a bag, and package it labelled as bread flour. I have been fortunate enough to get some freshly milled L.S. flour. It makes superb natural rise bread based on wheat-sprout enriched leaven.

Topline Bakers Wholemeal is available from Lowans. It is not organically grown, but is a good wholemeal bread flour.

Old Grain Mill Wholemeal W.I.   Lowans market flour under the label

'The Old Grain Mill' in supermarkets; this Wholemeal W.I. is generally suitable for bread, but has a very coarse bran content, inhibiting a high rise. This flour is suitable for sifting into a good 80 to 85 per cent flour.

Lowans Unbleached Bread Flour   One bag I bought recently was creamy in colour, with a wheaty aroma, and made exceptional bread. I have had other batches which were greyish and without such an aroma. They still produced good bread, however, and this flour is very useful. It makes creamy white bread and mixes well with wholemeals. Unbleached white flour should be ordered as it is only marketed in 20 kilo bags. One occasionally finds a health food store which carries it. Unbleached white flour is a non-injurious alternative for those who like 'white' bread or lighter than wholemeal. I like it more as a change or a treat, but the children love it. (See Glossary.)

Lowans also market an extensive range of non-wheat flours and meals in 1 kilo packs. These are generally available from health food or natural food stores. Included in their range are barley, oat, rye, buckwheat and brown rice flours, millet meal and polenta or corn meal. Lowan's flours are available in Tasmania where, to my knowledge, no wheat is grown locally, and no local flour marketed commercially. Tasmania could grow interesting wheat of the soft variety, similar to English wheat.

Salce Bros in Melbourne market an extremely high quality organic flour, ground on authentic granite stones in a traditional manner. They market 100 per cent wholemeal wheat, rye flours and a fine wheat flour. This flour is sold in larger natural food stores, such as Ceres and Soulfoods in Melbourne.

Biodynamic flour is available from McAdam Square Bulk Health Foods, Croydon, Victoria. In NSW, it is widely distributed as *Demeter* through health food and natural food stores along with their range of grain meals. Demeter is an international symbol signifying biodynamic quality. It is an excellent wholemeal, ground from Falcon variety wheat which is grown biodynamically. It is the best quality flour available though a little coarsely ground and the finest tasting wholemeal I have encountered.

Waterwheel market some flours in 10 kilo packages through super-markets. Their flour is also available through health food distributors and bakery suppliers. Quantities could be a problem. It's no use telephoning them and asking for 1 kilo of unbleached white flour! I believe this firm intends to market a flour labelled *Unbleached White Baker's Flour* through commercial outlets, which would definitely be an advance for the home baker. Their *50 per cent Wholemeal B5*, which is a blend of white flour and wholemeal, makes a good loaf and is suitable for blending with other flours. Waterwheel *100 per cent Wholemeal Wheat Flour* is a good wholemeal bread flour and, again, is excellent to blend.

D.G. Watson of Bordertown, SA, market an excellent wholemeal flour, milled from organic wheat, which is available in Adelaide. It is a good bread flour and is a more suitable grind or texture than other organic wholemeal flours available in Adelaide. *4 Leaf Farms* of Tarlee, SA, market a beautifully flavoured, biodynamically grown wholemeal wheat flour. It is coarsely ground and best used for heavier loaves or blending. Several shops in Adelaide, such as 'The Farmhouse' carry this flour which is not conventionally packaged or labelled.

Idly Wild is an unusual name and, to my knowledge, is the only chemical-free stoneground wholemeal available in Perth. It can be bought through a number of outlets, such as Ceres Wholefoods in Fremantle. Other commercial, roller-milled flours are available, such as *W. Thomas & Co's 88 per cent Atta Flour*. I have not tried this, but it sounds interesting. Atta is a wholemeal flour used for Indian chapatti (flat bread). It has the coarsest bran sifted out.

Oasis Stoneground Wholemeal is available from Toowong Trading Co. in Brisbane. I have not tried it. *Defiance Flour Mills* in Queensland produce a wholemeal which feels like a re-mix of roller-milled wheat and is without distinction, except that it has a high gluten content.

Quantity and Quality of Flours

An insurmountable difficulty, when setting out a bread recipe, is how to measure the quantity of flour as opposed to the quantity of liquids to be used. There are many brands of flour available commercially, all milled from wheat of varying quality. The climate, the season, the variety, the method of grinding and the age of the flour all affect the amount of liquid which can be used in the dough. Even if one always buys the same brand of flour, it can differ, depending on the supply of wheat. The miller may not be able to maintain a steady supply of grain from one source, and will buy in what is available. Hence a brand of flour may suddenly vary. Because of this, the quantities in bread recipes are only approximate, and recipes are most useful for their methodology. This is why, in order to be successful, the home baker must practise and learn the correct texture for the dough. This is not difficult but, unfortunately, often deters the timid, or those who are pressed for time. So be prepared to vary the quantity of flour specified and, if the texture does not seem correct, adjust it to satisfy your intuition, which is the best guide.

I have no doubt that the best wheat is organically grown and the best flour stoneground from such wheat. Its colour, flavour, aroma and effect on the final product are unmistakable — to me. Cynics will disagree, and that's fine — but they miss out on the romance which is part of our relationship with food. In a more practical vein, however, I have used inorganic flour which has killed my sensitive leavens. This may be due to a residue of chemicals from the processing — I cannot say with certainty.

Flour which has been grown and milled with integrity still retains the aroma of wheat. Heavily processed or chemicalised flour does not have this aroma. It can't be measured by any way other than by our human senses, so smell your flour. After a while, you will pick up the aromas or lack of them, and be able to detect freshness and quality with your divinely fallible senses. Grinding flour yourself from fresh, organic wheat will give you a standard — then go on to one of the commercial flour substitutes — you will soon know what I mean.

The argument as to whether organic or inorganic flour is best or even detectable does not warrant close attention here, neither does the question of using stoneground as opposed to roller milled. As a cook, one has license and I know what I like. Food should be a human concern, related to human desires and whims. To me, science, even nutrition, has a minimum role to play. The mental machinations involved with food are generally unnecessary — food is at gut level. Decide for yourself which is the best flour, but always remember there is no substitute for quality, especially when your food and consequent well-being are concerned.

Commercial white flour should be avoided; it is chemicalised and unbalanced, containing few of the most valuable nutrients and essences of wheat. For those of you who want lighter bread, unbleached white flour enriched with malt and oil is the answer. This fine textured flour is made by gradually sifting more and more bran and germ from the wholemeal. Commercial white flour has had almost every trace of bran and germ removed by sifting, and the residue destroyed by a bleaching process which gives it an artificial whiteness supposedly preferred by consumers. In most of the nations of Europe, flour is not permitted to be adulterated at all. Australia has no such laws. In England, it is required by law to replace those nutrients lost in bleaching and sifting, with artificial nutrients — of a pristine, whiter-than-white colour, not the 'degrading' earthy tones of wheat. How absurd that money, time and quality should be wasted by this bleaching and refining of flour, which is only necessitated by . . . what? Consumer demand? Decisions imposed by those who profit from this wasteful processing? The bakery factories which require flour to fit their mass-produced, profit-oriented, quality-less methods? Only bleached flour will withstand the violent mixing and short time processing of factory bread, where the dough must be matured rapidly, a process which is normally achieved by a fermentation of at least 4 hours. Bleaching artificially matures the flour, enabling quick handling and a sacrifice of quality for quantity. Perhaps in Australia, as in Europe, government legislation is necessary for consumer protection.

I do not believe that consumers have had much choice, as choice must come from alternatives. In the shops, there are very few alternatives to bread made from adulterated bread flours. How many of us have had the opportunity to compare bread made from chemicalised flour with the real thing? Even though a wide variety of bread seems to be available, most of the differences are cosmetic, based on the addition of gluten. Of the five rye loaves, three black breads, half a dozen wholemeals and a plethora of white loaves in a typical supermarket, perhaps three of them are really different. One can pick up a 'stoneground wholemeal' loaf expecting it to have some weight, and hurl it to the roof because of its surprising lightness. It weighs only 680 gm! A loaf of the same volume made with real flour weighs $1\frac{1}{2}$ to 2 kilos. Granted, reasonably good bread can be bought, but it is not widely available, and still does not bear comparison with the genuine, home-baked article.

The basic criteria for choice are flavour, which derives from materials and techniques, and health. Few have been fortunate enough to experience the flavour of fresh bread made with quality ingredients and baked in a wood-fired oven. Health is a huge problem. Many complaints have been associated with the consumption of refined flour and anyone who denies that chemicalised and refined flour is less wholesome and healthful than the natural product is deluded and out of touch with their intuitive discrimination. Many nutritionists will argue that chemical white flour is all right, provided the stripped nutrients are replaced. This may be true in scientific terms, but we, who are the playing fields of the nutritional game, are more than an agglomeration of chemicals. We are. We have human senses and feelings. Such senses dictate that whole is more wholesome than part . . . especially when the part, i.e. white flour, is subjected to chemical treatment. I am by no means attributing the ills of society to refined and chemicalised flour — I do in private — but I believe it would be a money-saving, quality-enhancing move if such flour were replaced by unbleached flour.

Most flour is roller milled. That is, wheat is forced into rollers which rotate at high speed. These shear open the wheat and separate its components. A roller-milled wholemeal is one in which the bran and germ have been mixed back in with bleached white flour after separation during the milling process. During baking, these behave quite differently from stoneground wholemeals and are less manageable in my experience. The process of roller milling has been attacked on many grounds. Its introduction made an immense impact on bread. For example, it necessitated the sifting of germ out of the flour because the high speed milling produced temperatures which made the germ go rancid, particularly with the harder wheats. Cooler operating roller mills have since been invented, but these are not generally in use. So, for convenience of processing in large quantities and storing, for mass-marketing and inevitably greater profits, denatured flour was foisted on the public.

Stoneground flour is always more manageable, smells better and looks better in the end product than roller milled flour. That's my judgement after experimenting. You may make your own decision.

Flours which have a large proportion of the bran and a small proportion (if any) of the germ extracted are called 80 per cent, 81 per cent, 85 per cent or by other names including unbleached. They are suitable bread flours if milled from the correct wheat and it is a good idea to make bread from such flours as they are nutritious and easily digestible. One hundred per cent wholemeal is not everyone's choice. We find it marvellous to experience bread made from 100 per cent, 80 per cent, unbleached flour and various other mixtures. My everyday choice is wholemeal, with weekly treats of various breads made from lighter flours, especially in summer.

We nearly always buy flour milled from organically grown wheat. This does restrict our range, although I have had great success sifting down 100 per cent wholemeals to wonderful 80 per cent or 85 per cent bread flours. It is worth buying organic bread flours as long as the wheat and milling are of high quality. I have found that organic flours produce the best tasting and smelling bread. The integrity of their growth and handling is passed on; foods grown with integrity have a more wholesome quality, even if this is not measurable other than by one's senses.

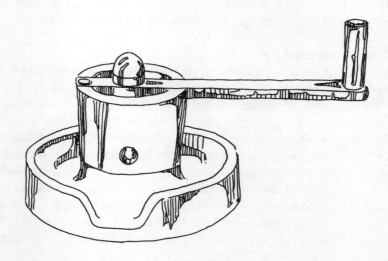

Grinding Your Own

The best bread, by my criteria, is made from freshly ground wheat. This is especially true of a leaven risen wholemeal, or near wholemeal. Even blending fresh wholemeal with unbleached white in different proportions enlivens the taste. Owning a grinder makes it possible to grind various meals which can be used in bread and which are not widely available. It is a boon to be able to use fresh oat flour or oatmeal, as this product very quickly goes rancid after grinding and has an unpleasant bitter flavour.

There are a few varieties of electric grinders available. They are often advertised in magazines devoted to health foods and natural lifestyles like *Simply Living*. Retsel and Samap make good ones. Samap also make an excellent stone hand-mill of ancient design, which is somewhat rigorous if more than a kilo or two of flour is required. Various other hand-operated grinders exist with metal burrs or synthetic stones. These are available from health food or natural food stores, or sometimes hardware stores. I use my electric grinder for stockfeed, porridge meal, and salt grinding as well as flour, so it earns its keep.

We buy a variety of wheat called 'Falcon'. This is biodynamically grown and is an exceptional bread wheat. Bread wheat should be coloured dark brown or reddish and the grain should be slightly translucent like rice. For pastry, we buy organically grown wheat marketed by Lowan Wholefoods. This is usually plump and yellow, not at all like bread wheat. When grinding your own flour for bread, avoid too fine or coarse a texture. Pastry flour should be ground as finely as the grinder can tolerate. It can be sifted if required.

If you haven't a grinder, be on the lookout for natural food and health food stores offering a flour grinding service.

Sifting Wholemeal Flour

One hundred per cent wholemeal, stoneground wheat flour can be sifted with good results, if it is not too coarsely ground. This will result in approximately 85 per cent flour, from which the coarsest bran has been removed. If you use a good strong wholemeal, like Lowan's 'L.S.' wholemeal, or one ground from Falcon wheat, for example, the result will be a strong wheat flour the like of which can't be purchased in Australia to my knowledge. The 80 per cent or 85 per cent wholemeal flours available are ground from soft wheat and are mainly used as pastry and cake flour. Sifting a roller milled wholemeal will result in bleached white flour, so make sure you use a stoneground wholemeal. Wholemeal rye flour can also be sifted to produce a light rye flour which makes excellent light rye bread when mixed with un-bleached white flour.

A suitable sifter with a fine gauze is required. These are available from many Chinese provision stores and more expensive ones from kitchen supply shops.

Flour Temperature

It is important that flour is not cold when used in a recipe. Usually, it is enough to add warm water to the dough to provide optimum temperature for the yeast to start multiplying. During winter however, it may be worth warming the flour in the oven. Place it in a bowl, cover with a plate or foil and set in a low oven for 5 minutes or until barely warm.

Dough Temperature

It is critical for professional bakers to keep dough temperatures within specified limits for the adequate performance of yeast and for the time-tabling of a bakery operation. It is not so critical at home, although you will have most success if you are aware of the appropriate temperatures. After a while, this becomes second nature and a thermometer is not really necessary. Bakers would keep a short-term dough between 24-26°C (76-78°F). A 6-hour dough is maintained between 22-23°C (74-75°F). At home, simply ensure the dough is not cooler than 24°C (76°F) for a standard operation. The initial Scotch-bake dough (Recipe 35), for example, can be mixed without too much concern as its first fermentation is 8 to 12 hours. When checked after this time, it will have warmed to 24°C (76°F) through fermentation. The second stage of fermentation sees the dough temperature rise to 27°C (80°F). It is then kept no lower than 26°C (78°F) for its final proving. These temperatures are useful because they indicate the range within which you can work and may help you to analyse faults in the final product.

Use of Grain Flours Other Than Wheat

It is extremely difficult to make a palatable risen bread in the European sense from any cereal other than wheat and rye. Breads made from 100 per cent non-wheat flours excluding rye, are usually made in ways that differ from the familiar tinning, rising and baking of Europe. Bread generally becomes heavier and rises less as the proportion of non-wheat flour in a dough is increased. The flours or fine meal of all cereals other than wheat can be used in a bread mix and will produce a delicious loaf if used in correct proportion with wheat flour. For explicit directions, please consult the appropriate recipe.

Some success can be had by the more experienced and adventurous at making 100 per cent barley bread on the sourdough leaven system. The unleavened 100 per cent barley bread of England and Wales is baked on a griddle or hot-plate. Injera, the 100 per cent millet bread of Africa, is cooked in a hot pan. Tortillas or tostadas, the corn bread of the Americas, is made Chapatti style.

The best all-round bread, made from non-wheat flour excluding rye, uses one-third flour or meal to two-thirds wheat flour. The proportion of non-wheat flour can be less — one-fifth still produces the flavour with a less crumbly loaf, but I prefer a stronger barley grain flavour, for example, and like these breads a little crumbly. The flour should not be too coarsely milled. I have found it best to use a meal of similar texture to wholemeal flour, although slightly coarser barley and oatmeal are all right. The type of wheat flour employed is important with regard to the heaviness and flavour of the finished product. One hundred per cent barley flour used with 100 per cent wholemeal wheat flour can produce a heavy and unpleasant loaf unless managed with care. One-third barley meal, one-third 100 per cent wholemeal wheat flour and one-third unbleached white produces a delightful, sweet smelling loaf in which the flavour of the barley is clear. The most delicious barley loaf is one-third fine barley flour and two-thirds unbleached white flour.

Generally, the mixtures I have found successful are: one-third rye, fine millet flour, cornmeal, oatmeal, buckwheat or barley, with one-third 100 per cent wholemeal wheat and one-third unbleached white or 80 per cent wheat flour. Brown rice flour works better in smaller proportions, no more than a quarter. Really the best way to incorporate rice into a loaf is to cook it as whole grain (Recipe 8). Bread made from one-third fine millet flour and two-thirds unbleached white has a hard, dark crisp crust and a most endearing flavour (Recipe 26).

Oatmeal in the flour mixture produces a moist and satisfying grain flavour. Care must be taken that the oatmeal or oat flour you use is not rancid. Smell and taste. If there is any bitter odour or flavour, the meal is rancid. This happens quickly with oats as they have a high fat content and it is better to use freshly ground whole oats.

Buckwheat bread is not at all common, but has a good flavour and aroma. Buckwheat can also be incorporated in bread as a cooked whole grain (Recipe 8). As buckwheat is a heating cereal, use it in winter.

Rye bread can be made from 100 per cent rye flour. It is black heavy and sour, with a satisfying savoury quality. It is made on a sourdough leaven system and is described in Recipe 14 and under leavens (page 41). Elderly Europeans used to come into the bakery in Melbourne after tasting our 100 per cent rye and exclaim that they had not tasted this bread since before World War Two and that it reminded them of their childhood . . . today's rye breads are mostly sad imitations of this invigorating and sustaining bread.

One hundred per cent rye flour does not necessarily mean that 100 per cent whole rye meal has been used, but it does mean that no wheat flour has been used. Rye flour is often sifted, producing a lighter bread. When whole rye meal is mixed half and half with unbleached white flour, a fine light rye results. The rye flours marketed by Lowans and by Salce Bros in Melbourne, and by Demeter in Sydney are 100 per cent whole rye meal. You can make light rye flour by sifting them. These flours are generally available in health food and natural food stores. At the time of writing, some firms which usually carry rye flour were unable to procure stocks, rye being in very short supply.

Unfortunately, salt today isn't worth its salt. It is usually a mixture of chemicals, which ensure its free-flowing quality, and chemically refined pure sodium-chloride. On a recent airline trip, I was given a sachet marked 'Salt'. The ingredients stated were salt, sodium silico aluminate, tri-calcium phosphate, dextrose, potassium iodide and polysorbate 80 . . . salt??? Iodised salt and free-flowing salt are unsuitable for bread baking and, in my opinion, human consumption.

Unrefined sea salt is the most suitable for all cooking and baking. This is because it has a less harsh flavour and effect on the dough than chemicalised salt. Further, the natural minerals held in combination with sodium chloride make natural sea salt a more balanced food.

The answer is to buy salt which is labelled 'Unrefined Pure Seasalt'. Health food shops carry one brand of French seasalt under the Russell's label. This is a grey salt and is merely evaporated sea water. It is highly suitable but, ridiculously, imported from France! Ceres Natural Foods, Chapel Street, Prahran, Victoria, have irregular supplies of a sea salt which is ground from washed, evaporated sea water. It is the most suitable salt I have used. Lowans market a good quality rock salt and, again, irregular supplies of 'Salt from the Sea' are available in some health food stores. This is an unrefined natural sea salt from New Zealand.

It is worth visiting a large-scale salt works. Ask for a sack of butter salt. This is washed, coarse granular salt. It needs to be ground, but is very cheap. There are varieties of rock salt, produced in Australia, which are of good quality. The only problem is the price compared with sea salt. But quality is worth paying for . . . to an extent. Some cooking salt available in supermarkets, for example the 'Pacific' brand, seems to be okay.

If you prefer to use no salt, I suggest leaven-risen breads. The question of salt and health is not one I want to go into here, except that I think it is very short sighted to blame salt for so much. Highly processed foods are loaded with heavily refined and chemicalised salt which is undoubtedly not wholesome. If you eat natural, traditional foods, well prepared, with a traditional balance, you have no reason to fear salt. This fear is rightly felt by those who choose to eat refined and chemicalised foods and who have a salt 'condition' because of that choice. Most vegetarians of some years standing can tolerate a higher proportion of salt than individuals who eat large quantities of red meat.

Salt Quantities
Yeasted bread is very insipid without a proper measure of salt. Also it is not a balanced food, because salt conditions the dough and tempers the yeast, thus making bread more digestible if properly chewed. Leaven risen bread requires about one-third the amount of salt that yeasted bread does. This is probably because the leaven itself conditions the dough through the production of acids resulting from the conversion of substances (e.g. carbohydrates) through enzymatic fermentation.

More salt is employed in tinned breads than in free standing loaves. This is because tinned breads tend to be softer doughs, containing more water than the dough for a free standing, crusty, Continental style loaf. A softer or more liquid dough needs the contracting action of salt to keep it at a useable texture as the dough matures. Crusty free standing loaves, especially slashed ones, need to be free to open up. Too much salt restricts freedom of movement. This principle is really demonstrated when larger amounts of flour are used as the quantity of salt varies about 500 gm per 68 kilo sack of flour for different types of bread.

Generally, longer maturing doughs require more salt than shorter time doughs, as salt slows the tendency of the dough to become soft or more liquid as it matures over a number of hours. The Scotch-bake bread (Recipe 35) is interesting in this respect, especially in the timing of the salt addition.

Salt Alternatives
Miso is a natural ferment of soya beans and grain, tempered by salt. It is available in natural food and health food stores. Use 1 tablespoon

in a 1 kilo loaf of leaven risen bread, or 3 tablespoons in a yeasted loaf (see Recipe 28). Of course, miso also contains salt, but the Oriental belief is that the salt is more easily metabolised due to its involvement in the complex bacterial fermentation of the miso. If you buy miso, be sure to buy a naturally fermented, chemical free product, such as those marketed by Spiral Foods, Russells or Westbrae.

Salt and Yeast

Salt and yeast are different sides of the same coin. Salt slows and tempers the action of yeast. It also improves the flavour of yeast in the end product. If you are leaving a dough for 2 or 3 provings, perhaps overnight for full maturation, leave the amount of salt as usual, but decrease the amount of yeast. For a quick rise, use the standard amount of salt, but increase the yeast quantity slightly.

WATER AND OTHER LIQUIDS

Water is the primary liquid for making bread. Its quality can vastly affect the finished product to the extent of killing the leaven or producing a superior loaf. On one occasion, when making bread in unusual circumstances, I used water which smelled so strongly of chlorine I could not envisage leaven surviving — but it did. This bread had poor volume, however, and staled rapidly. On other occasions, notably in Adelaide, I have had leaven killed stone dead by the water. As it is approximately one-third of your bread, try to use good quality water. Soft water supposedly produces a loaf of better volume than hard water. Soft water from a rainwater tank is preferable to water from a softwater system. I am using crystal clear spring and river water at the time of writing, and this enhances the natural wheat flavour. Most of you will have no choice but to turn on the tap and knead away, so remember water as a factor when analysing failure, particularly with leavens.

Water should be lukewarm or a little hotter for winter bread baking, but never too hot, as this will kill the yeast and alter the dough unfavourably. Water at room temperature is adequate for summer. Cold water slows down the rising process, which is an advantage in summer, when dough can rise too fast and not benefit from slow maturation.

I do not use oil or milk in my leaven breads; this is a matter of dietary preference. However, an excellent bread can be made, incorporating milk or yoghurt in a leaven based bread, particularly cow's milk or soymilk in a sourdough made from unbleached white flour. Yeasted bread benefits from the addition of other liquids besides water, although this is not essential. Loaves enriched with oil, tofu, butter, cream or milk are a treat. Everyday bread is based on water.

Oil
The reason for adding oil to a dough is to improve its texture. The dough becomes lighter and easier to work and the bread softer, with a

well-rounded flavour. It is worth using in yeasted bread, particularly bread made from unbleached white flour, or with a large proportion of it. I use unrefined, cold-pressed oil, finding refined oil a bland and possibly unwholesome commodity. My choice is virgin olive oil. Pure, unrefined light sesame oil is also very good, as are some brands of Chinese peanut oil, which are not reduced to a tasteless, odourless and colourless liquid. If you can possibly afford, and procure it, hazelnut oil makes unforgettable bread. Corn, sunflower and safflower oils all have a flavour which I do not appreciate in bread. You may enjoy the sunflower flavour, however, and other oils may not be available to you — so experiment. Good quality Greek and Italian oils are widely available in Australia — ask for virgin first pressing — you might be lucky. Spiral Foods market a beautiful Italian olive oil under the name Santa Sabina. Good quality virgin olive oil is available in SA and some interstate continental groceries and markets, such as Prahran market in Melbourne. Some of it is produced in various small extraction plants by the Greek and Italian communities in Adelaide. Cheaper alternatives are Spanish olive oil from the supermarket, which is satisfactory.

As oil inhibits yeast to an extent, incorporate it after the first rising, or later as in the Scotch-bake recipe (Recipe 35). If using only one rise or proving before baking, incorporate the oil in the initial mixture. In this case, blend oil with the water to form an emulsion. Another way of adding oil is to pour it onto the kneading surface and work it into the dough as you knead. Be sure to do this thoroughly. This method is most suitable for adding oil after the first or second proving for a longer maturing dough. Alternatively, oil can be rubbed into the flour. Generally, use 3 to 4 tablespoons of oil per kilo of flour.

Oil can be liberated by finely grinding sunflower or sesame seeds, or nuts such as hazel, peanut or cashew. Toast the nuts or seeds in the oven until they are fragrant and lightly coloured. If they are then ground while warm, more oil is available. An electric blender or coffee mill is suitable as a grinder. When this fine meal is rubbed into the flour, the dough becomes smoother, characteristic of the effect of oil on a dough. Another benefit is the fine flavour which these meals add. If you use seed or nut meal, it is not necessary to add any extra oil. Meals of this kind are suitable for salty or sweet bread. Quantities: 2 cups of meal per 1 kilo of flour. Tahina or sesame puree can also be used instead of oil. Use 2 tablespoons per 1 kilo of flour and rub it in, or preferably puree with the water. This is very successful in wholemeal wheat yeast bread.

Cow's Milk and Other Milks

Cow's milk produces a soft, high, flavoursome loaf when used as part of a liquid ingredient. I do not use cow's milk at all, finding soymilk a preferable and perhaps more healthful 'milk'. If you choose to use cow's milk in bread, it is best to use it half and half with water. Rolls can be made with 100 per cent milk if desired, and these are a delicious treat. Cream can also be added, especially to wholemeal yeasted bread, producing a moist loaf.

Soymilk is an excellent, if unorthodox liquid to use in yeasted breads. It can be made at home* or purchased in small sachets from natural food and health food stores. It is distributed by Spiral Foods and is called 'Bon-Soy'. Soymilk sold in Asian groceries usually contains refined cane sugar.

Coconut milk can be made fresh or purchased in a can from Asian food stores. Be sure to buy the unsweetened variety. To make fresh coconut milk, grate the white flesh of a coconut. Place in a bowl and mix with a little more than its volume of water. Squeeze vigorously for a few minutes until the water becomes very milky. Strain off the grounds and squeeze again to extract all the milk. It is now ready to be used in bread and, incidentally, is an essential liquid in authentic curries or south-east Asian dishes like Gado-Gado or Satay. Coconut milk makes the bread much softer than other milks.

Tofu

Soya bean curd called Tofu by the Japanese and Dow Foo by the Chinese is another unorthodox but successful addition. It should be pureed first and added as one would add cream. This makes very good bread with a moist texture, a soft crust and an excellent protein profile. Four tablespoons of pureed tofu per 1 kilo flour is enough for yeasted bread made with wholemeal wheat flour, although much larger quantities can be used for softer bread and cakes (see Recipes 9, 32 and 33). Tofu is available from natural food stores, Chinese and Japanese grocers. Morinaga brand silken tofu is pre-packaged and has a long unrefrigerated shelf life. It is convenient and widely available. Fresh tofu is best, however[‡].

Other Liquid Ingredients

Many modern bread makers use molasses or honey in their bread,

---

* See *Natural Tucker*, chapter 12, by John Downes (Hyland House, Melbourne) for instructions.

‡ Instructions for making tofu can be found in *Natural Tucker*, chapter 12.

believing them to be healthful, or perhaps because they enhance the yeast activity. Molasses and honey certainly stimulate the yeast activity and they may be healthful; I personally abhor both of them in bread, unless it is a specialty bread. Molasses overshadows all in terms of flavour and honey, if of any quality and not refined to merely a sweet syrup, is always evident in the aroma and taste of a loaf. Honey contributes to a moist and longer keeping bread. I prefer to use various fruit juices, notably apple and grape, in specialty breads. These will produce a mild sweetness or enhance the natural sweetness of a little maple syrup or honey, and they enable you to avoid using refined cane sugar.

Liquid malt is a valuable bread ingredient as long as it is not used excessively. Again it can overpower all other tastes. A small quantity of liquid or dried malt (pure powder) improves dough texture, especially the crust. Too much produces a cloying flavour and bread which is too heavy or moist, because the malt has thinned the dough. Malt is a useful addition to rye leavens and rye bread, producing better volume in the loaf.

LEAVENING AGENTS

Sourdough or Natural-rise Leaven

This is the most ancient method used to leaven bread and, in my opinion, produces the best flavour, nutrition and satisfaction. The natural-rise sourdough system was used, in one form or another, as the principle method of leavening bread, until the last century. Different nationalities developed many variations to produce their own style of leaven and bread. In various parts of Europe this system is still in everyday use. I have been told that some bakeries in Brittany still produce the most delicious 'pain brie' (not the cheese) with natural leaven and such bread is also available in Eastern Europe.

Depending on the leaven and its management, the flavour of natural-rise bread can be sour, yeast-like or redolent of wheat. Sourdough bread is the name given to a natural-rise bread which has a distinctly sour, pleasant flavour. Some varieties of natural-rise bread I have tried have a more wheat-like flavour. It depends on what the leaven is fed and which particular varieties of wild yeast(s) it contains. Flemish bakers produced a leaven they called 'desem' which was strong in its rise and barely sour. This was grown in cool surrounds, too much warmth promoting the sour flavour. I have successfully maintained a similar starter for five or six years now.

Natural-rise starters are claimed to have significant health benefits. Whether these benefits can be scientifically identified, I don't know, but bread made from them is certainly invigorating. It is claimed that the significant quantity of calcium in wheat, which is supposedly not normally available to the human system, is made assimilable by these natural leavens. This happens through the hydrolisation of certain acids. Further, it seems that a wide spectrum of B group vitamins, especially B12, are available in natural-rise breads which are made without additives.

I am the proud possessor of a hundred year old sourdough culture given to me in dried form by an American friend. I was told that the settlers and miners in the Yukon would leave a bowl of flour and water paste under certain berry shrubs. These shrubs attracted or imparted certain yeasts which produced the very best sourdough. Men in those parts were known by the quality of their sourdough! The one I have is supposedly one of the very best ever to have been caught under a Yukon berry bush, and is very active and delicious.

Making a Leaven

Begin with the best quality flour. It should be organically grown and freshly ground. Experience has taught me that this definitely produces the most active and flavoursome leaven. Use the cleanest available water. I have had leavens killed by chemicals in both flour and water.

Ingredients: 2 cups wholemeal wheat flour and 3 cups water. Mix the flour with water to produce about $^3/_4$ litre of medium consistency batter. It should have no lumps. Place in a glass or earthenware bowl, cover with a cotton cloth and leave for 2 to 5 days until bubbles appear and the batter is obviously active. There may be a slight sour odour. Mix this with the same quantity of flour and water and allow it to ferment again. The leaven is now ready to use. A portion of it is mixed with more flour, water and salt to produce a dough which will rise. Use most of the leaven when making the bread and mix the remaining cupful or so with more flour and water — back to the batter consistency. Store in a jar and keep refrigerated. When required for use, it can be left to stand for an hour or so to warm up and then mixed into the dough, once again retaining a cupful. In this way, the starter is maintained indefinitely. If you don't have success with this technique, it may be due to variations in climate, flour and water. Keep trying and use different places to grow leaven until the right coincidence of factors occurs.

Leaven is far easier to grow in wholemeal than in white or 80 per cent flours. Naturally, wholemeal has a more satisfactory range of nutrients for it. You will find the leaven process works best when the same flour is used for both the leaven and the bread, although this is not a hard and fast rule. Very interesting bread can be made with unbleached white flour and a wholemeal leaven. A leaven can be started in 80 per cent or unbleached white flour by using a little wholemeal starter, but should be continued with whichever flour is being used for the bread. Unbleached white flour leaven usually needs to be fed with wheat sprouts or liquid malt fortnightly.

Leavens in Non-Wheat Flours

One hundred per cent barley bread can be made on the leaven system.

Mix 1 tablespoon of your usual wheat leaven with a batter made from 100 per cent barley flour and water. This will activate the barley batter, just as it does the wheat batter, which can be mixed with more flour, water and salt to produce a dough which will rise and can be baked in the same manner as wheat bread.

By mixing 1 tablespoon of leaven into a batter of millet flour and water, you make the basis for the north African bread, Injera. This is cooked as a thick pancake. It is quite sour and unusual, a perfect accompaniment to bean stews or soups.

Rye Leaven

Follow the same process as for making a wheat leaven, except 100 per cent rye flour is used. It can be activated by a wheat leaven. To do this, add 1 tablespoon leaven to $1/2$ litre (1 pint) batter of rye flour and water. Some old recipes recommend a single slice of raw onion in the batter. I use more leaven when making rye bread than wheat bread. It produces a strongly flavoured, dark, moist loaf which keeps for three weeks. Crushed, five day old rye sprouts are the best food for a rye leaven (see page 43 under Keeping leavens).

Rye leaven mixed with wheat flour to make a dough results in an excellent bread. This entails mixing a rye leaven into unbleached white flour for a light rye, or into wholemeal for a heavier bread.

Malt Leaven

Liquid malt or pure light malt powder produces a very active leaven. Add 1 teaspoon malt liquid or pure malt powder (sometimes called light crystal malt) to 1 litre of leaven.

Fruit Leaven

Fruit leaven is a wheat flour leaven with the addition of fermented fruit juice. Press or juice apples to make 550 ml (1 pint) of juice. Place the juice in a glass or pottery bowl, set in a warm place and cover with a cotton cloth. In 2 to 5 days, fermentation will occur. When this is at its most vigorous, mix in enough fresh, wholemeal wheat flour and a little water to produce a batter. Cover with a cloth and wait till it activates by bubbling and frothing. Use as a standard leaven (see Recipes 52 and 56). Fruit leavens can be made with other varieties of fermented fruit, such as freshly squeezed grapes.

Grain Leaven

Left-over, cooked brown rice is ideal to start this ferment. Allow the rice to stand at room temperature in a bowl covered by a cotton cloth

until it smells faintly sweet — the first stage of what some would call
'going off '. Mix with water and fresh wholemeal flour to a batter consistency. The mixture should be active within 1 day. Proceed in the
usual manner by adding flour, water and salt to make a dough. Tin,
rise, bake.

Miso Enriched Leaven

Although not contributing to the activity of the leaven, miso (fermented soya bean paste) can be added for extra flavour and nutrition.
Use one teaspoon per 550 ml (1 pint) of leaven and add in the same
quantity each time the leaven is renewed.

However, I do not recommend making leavens on the basis of
legume fermentation, e.g. soured beans, as toxic substances are likely
to result.

Wheat Starch Leaven

When making wheat gluten*, an ingredient in some Asian cooking,
the starch is washed out of a dough made from unbleached white flour
and water. This leaves the gluten or protein which is further cooked. If
the washed-out starch is allowed to stand for an hour or two and most
of the remaining water poured off, a batter results. This can be used to
great advantage as a thickening agent for sauces or can be left in a
warm place to ferment. This may only take one day in warm weather.
The fermented batter is then mixed with flour, water and salt to
produce a bread dough which is tinned, risen and baked.

Hops Leaven

Boil 14 to 15 gm (1/2 oz) yellow hops in 1.14 litres (1 quart) water for
1/2 hour. Cool to room temperature. Strain. Mix in fresh, wholemeal
wheat flour to form a batter and 1 teaspoon liquid dark malt or 1 cup
crushed five day old rye sprouts. This becomes very active in 2 to 3
days and can be used at its peak or stored in the refrigerator for up to 2
months. Make up into bread as in leaven recipes.

Special Baking Ferment

If all your attempts at making a home grown leaven are unsuccessful,
or you don't have the time, it is possible to buy a very high quality
leaven starter from Helios Enterprises at the Demeter Bakery, 65
Derwent Street, Glebe, Sydney. This baking ferment is chemical and
yeast free. It is evidently grown from cereal grain and honey. The ferment is manufactured in Germany and the only identification of its

* See *Natural Tucker*, chapter 12.

producer is D-6364, Florstadt-1, Germany. It is an excellent starter for leaven based bread, giving a good rise and a barely sour, wheat-enhancing flavour. Mix one heaped tablespoon of the ferment powder with 200 gm of wholemeal wheat flour. Add 1 cup of water and mix well. It is best to use a non-metal bowl for the mixing. Cover with a plate and leave in a warm place to activate for 24 hours. When it is bubbling and frothy, mix with 300 gm of wholemeal wheat flour and enough water to make a thick batter, rather the same as has been described under Making a leaven (see page 40). Leave this for another 24 hours to activate. It is now ready for use and is best used at this stage because, as with all leavens, it acquires characteristic acidity or sourness with age. This is not bad, it is just that the most delicious bread results from a leaven used at its peak of activity. Use the leaven as directed in the recipes. It is renewed by adding fresh flour and water to the remaining leaven and should be refrigerated or cellared immediately for future use.

Keeping Leavens

The best place for a leaven is a refrigerator or a cold, dark cellar. A general rule seems to be that the older and more mature a leaven, the sourer it is. This is usually agreeable as the 'sourdough' flavour, but can become excessive and unpleasant. If your leaven becomes too sour, pour off all but 1 tablespoon and refresh with more flour and water. Make sure you grow the leaven in a glass or earthenware bowl and cover with a cotton cloth. Refrigerate or cellar it immediately so it will activate slowly. This reduces the sourness. As soon as a refreshed leaven is noticeably active, it should be used so that you get a good flavour and maximum rise. Generally leaven kept in a warm place becomes sour rapidly and rising in too warm a place causes a sour flavour in leaven risen bread and a tendency towards a dough which is too sticky or liquid.

Once you have made a leaven, it can be improved through being fed the right foods, as we all can. Feeding only needs to be done once a month or less, if the leaven is being used continuously. The best leaven food is complex carbohydrate. I have found five day old wheat sprouts to be ideal. Simply crush the wheat sprouts in a mortar or suribachi* and mix 1 cup wheat sprouts to 1 litre leaven. This produces an active fermentation and a sweet, wheatlike flavour. Leaven can also be fed on cooked brown rice or barley. Cook the whole cereal in the usual manner. Cool. Knead 1 cup of rice or barley with 3 cups of water until the water is milky. Add the lot to the leaven

* Japanese mortar with a grooved bowl.

and thicken with flour to produce the required batter consistency. I usually alternate wheat sprouts and rice as leaven foods to maintain flavour and activity.

Some use refined cane sugar to 'sweeten' their leavens. This is detrimental to the leavens as it kills certain nutrients and spoils the pleasant acidity of the bread. Apart from that, why spoil a natural leaven with a highly refined carbohydrate such as cane sugar? It has no place in bread and the best bread is made without it.

Making Grain Sprouts

It is important to use organic or biodynamic wheat or rye for sprouting. Soak wholewheat or rye for 24 hours. Strain off the water, which can be mixed into bread dough or used to make a leaven. Place the grains in a 5 cm (2 inch) deep pan or bowl made of stainless steel or plastic. Cover with a wet cotton cloth. Every day cover with water, let stand for a few minutes, then pour the water off. Re-cover and leave in a dark place, for example a cupboard or pantry. In 5 days, the sprouts will be a mat of fibre and suitable for using in leavens or breads and for making Essene Bread (Recipe 41). 750 gm is an appropriate quantity of wheat to soak. This gives 1.5 kilos of sprouts, plenty for everyday use. They can be stored in the refrigerator for up to 7 days.

Leaven Contamination

This does not mean that the leaven may become a danger to your health, but that commercial yeast has taken over due to contamination in the kitchen. The contamination is obvious from a pronounced yeasty odour and over active leaven.

This can be caused by not cleaning bowls and utensils properly. If you want to make leaven-risen bread and yeast bread at the same time, don't even take the yeast out of the refrigerator until all the leaven bread is tinned. In this way, there is less danger of contamination.

A leaven which has been taken over by a commercial yeast will return to its previous quality after continual refreshment. For a soured starter use the procedure described on page 43 under Keeping leavens. The commercial yeast will slowly be taken over by your original culture. Usually a leaven which has been left refrigerated for 2 months can also be re-activated by this method, even if quite sour. If the starter has mould on the surface, simply remove it and use a little of the remaining mould-free starter in a new batter. Obviously, a putrid smelling 'starter' is beyond help, but generally leavens exhibit remarkable powers of recovery.

Barm or Beer Yeast

The ancient Egyptians were renowned bakers; the leaven they used was a by-product of making beer. Beer-making and bread baking have gone hand in hand for thousands of years, beer yeast being used throughout Europe until the last century when our now-familiar compressed yeast was found to be more reliable. It is well worth making bread from barm or beer yeast as the flavour is excellent, far better than today's commercial yeast.

Barm has attributes both of a sourdough-style leaven, and yeast. Barm accentuates the wheat flavour and has only slight acidity. The dough ripens and rises in a yeast-like fashion, although usually not with quite as much volume. The texture of the finished bread has the quality of a leaven dough, boosted with yeast. Barm dough reacts to warmth in the same way as a yeast dough, so keep it slightly warm as with yeast — a little warmer than a leaven dough.

Barm doughs need to be baked at yeast temperatures — usually 220-230°C (425-450°F) whereas leaven breads are baked at lower temperatures. Barm bread needs 45 minutes for a 1 kilo tin loaf. Leaven needs to be baked for 1 hour.

Recipes which are written specifically for barm such as Barm-brack (Recipe 44) are not the same if made with yeast. The colour, odour and texture are different — although still good eating! Leaven and barm can be interchanged with similar results, except that barm produces a greater 'kick' or rise in the first 10 minutes of baking.

The beer yeast I use comes from beer brewed in South Australia, known as Coopers Ale and exported as Coopers Real Ale. This is a naturally brewed beer and contains a sediment. When the beer is consumed, pour the sediment into an earthenware bowl and mix with flour and water to form a thick batter. Cover with a cloth and leave to ferment overnight. When ready it will bubble and froth and can then be used as a rising agent in the same way as a leaven, and in the same quantities.

Renew the barm with fresh flour and water to a thick batter consistency and refrigerate in a sealed container. Before use, put in a warm spot until it reaches room temperature. Renew the barm weekly, as it does not have the keeping quality of leavens. This can be done with a new infusion of sediment from the beer.

As I brew beer regularly, I have opportunity to use barm. It's very simple to buy a home-brew kit with completely natural ingredients, add water and yeast, ferment and bottle. Maple syrup, honey, palm sugar or maltose can be used in place of the suggested white cane sugar for bottling. The yeast which accumulates on the surface of the beer liquid as it brews, mixed with a little wort (malt), produces an active sponge when flour and water are added. The flavour is a little better than the yeast from the bottom of a bottle of beer. But this can only be made by those of you who brew beer . . . Even if you don't drink the beer, buy a stubby of Coopers, wash your hair with it, and keep the sediment for bread.

Scottish bakers made an excellent barm by using a malt extract or wort. The latter liquid is produced by boiling roasted, crushed barley sprouts in water and is the basic liquid in beer.

Commercial Yeast — Compressed and Dried

Compressed yeast can be bought by weight in a block from the delicatessen department of supermarkets, from continental grocers and from health food shops. It is very reliable, easy to use and has a better flavour than dried yeast. In my experience, it always produces a less dry bread. Keep it sealed and refrigerated. I have kept it this way for 2 months before it went mouldy.

There is a great temptation, because of its form as granules, to use dried yeast in excess and this produces too strong a rise and consequently crumbly, unmanageable bread. In general, use half as much dried yeast as compressed yeast. Whether using dried or compressed yeast, the rule is to use the minimum quantity. More yeast does not produce a better rise, just a bigger one. Time is what produces the best rise and texture. When using commercial yeast, it is best to start with a small portion of yeast and leave the dough to mature over a day and night, knocking it back (punching down) several times as the yeast grows. The flavour, texture and keeping quality of the bread is far improved by using the minimum yeast and maximum maturation.

I prefer bread made without commercial yeast as it is more nourishing, flavourful and sustaining. Yeasted bread is a somewhat cosmetic luxury for me, although it is the most popular today. It takes time to acquire a taste for, and the patience to chew, heavier, natural-rise breads. Some believe that commercial yeast is not a good food for man and that it is a root cause of cancer and other modern, degenerative diseases. It was certainly treated with great suspicion when introduced to Europe in the eighteenth and nineteenth centuries. I notice that after being a sourdough (natural-rise) bread eater for many years, eating yeasted bread, even from the best ingredients, leaves me craving for something more sustaining.

Yeast Quantities

The quantity of yeast to be used varies with the type of bread you are making and your time. If you are very busy and think a lengthy fermentation is not possible, consider maturing the dough overnight or during the day while at work. Dough does not have to be watched; you need spend only 15 minutes working on it during the whole process. A dough can be made in the morning with a small amount of yeast, left all day to prove, and then be re-mixed (knocked down, or punched back) in the afternoon, tinned, risen and baked (see Recipe 17). Such bread has a better flavour than bread made from go to whoa in 2 or 3 hours with a larger proportion of yeast. It also fits well into busy schedules. 5-10 gm of yeast is sufficient for 1 kilo of flour if you prove for 8 hours or more. A faster-rising, short time bread can be made from 25-35 gm of yeast per kilo of flour. If using dried yeast, use 5 gm in the first instance and 15 gm in the second. Too much yeast definitely spoils the texture, flavour and keeping quality of a loaf. This is not to say however, that one cannot make a better bread in 1½ hours than can be bought commercially — anywhere.

Baking

Although it is inevitable that some people have to cook with electricity, I consider it the least desirable cooking medium. To a certain extent, it denatures food. Microwave just isn't cooking. Gas is the best alternative to wood, which is ideal but perhaps not universally practical. There is a great deal of difference between these three ways of cooking. The results of baking and the methodology to be used, to a certain extent, vary. Domestic ovens are in any case very idiosyncratic and you must take this into consideration when baking and setting temperatures. Older style ovens of heavier construction inevitably maintain their heat better and are better for baking in general.

Of course, the ideal oven for baking bread is the Scotch, or side-firing oven, or its European counterpart, in which the fire is lit in the oven and later raked out. The bread is baked in a steamy atmosphere, as these ovens can be sealed up, and the heat which is radiated from the bricks forms a superb crust. Because this oven bakes with a clear-radiated heat, the bread flavour is cleaner and more distinctive. Often these old brick ovens are now fired by oil, but this creates a toxic residue in which the bread is baked.

Unless there are other instructions, preheat the oven to the required temperature. Ensure that the oven is not crowded with too many tins, as this will reduce the initial baking temperature which is so important for a good oven 'kick' (the loaf rises or 'kicks' a few centimetres) and the initial setting of the dough. It is interesting to note that tinned bread made on a leaven does not kick or rise in the oven as a result of the initial exposure to high heat as much as bread leavened with commercial yeast. Yeasted bread can spring up 5-10 cm, whereas a 1-2 cm kick is characteristic of sourdough or leaven-risen breads.

Place the loaves in the middle or upper section of the oven to ensure they benefit fully from the heat. If necessary, change the position of the loaves to ensure even baking — most ovens have hot and cold spots. This should not be done before the bread has baked 15 minutes.

	Yeast	*Barm*	*Leaven*
Final prove in tin or shape	1 hour	3 hours	6 hours
Baking temperature	220-230°C (425-450°F)	220°C (425°F)	205°C (400°F)
Length of bake	35-45 minutes	45 minutes	1 hour

Baking Times and Temperatures

I bake yeasted bread for 35 minutes in a hot oven 220°C (425°F) or 45 minutes in a slower oven 205°C (400°F). The hot oven is better for white and lighter yeasted breads, while the moderate oven is better for 100 per cent wholemeal. Baking in a moderate oven can be extended to an hour if you are not satisfied with the result. Bread raised on a leaven benefits from an even baking temperature. I usually bake the natural-rise bread at 205°C (400°F) for 1 hour or 1¹/₂ hours for large (1.5 kilo) loaves. Barm bread responds to similar temperatures and times as yeast, although perhaps a little cooler, say 210°C (415°F), and a little longer, 45 minutes as opposed to the 35 to 40 minutes for yeasted breads.

As I am accustomed to baking in a wood-fired oven, commercially and at home, I do not have the opportunity to manipulate baking temperatures and, for example, reduce the heat for the last phase of baking. This results in interesting bread for us, sometimes very crusty. However, good results can be had from an initial bake for yeasted bread of 220°C (425°F) for 15 minutes, then reducing the heat to 205°C (400°F) for the remaining 15 to 30 minutes. Some of these times are less than precise, I realise; however, baking is not a sterile, scientific operation and baking times can vary by 15 minutes! Enjoy the variety and remember that overcooked is preferable to undercooked.

I recommend untinning loaves and returning them to the oven for 3 to 5 minutes to ensure a good crust and to clear excess moisture resulting from being in a tin. It is, of course, impossible to untin a loaf if the tin has not been adequately oiled, see page 51. Do a thorough job to save the heartbreak of digging a superb loaf out of a tin.

When the bread is untinned and has had its final bake, remove it from the oven and place on a wire cooling rack. Do not wrap it and make sure there are no strong cooling draughts. Bread is best left 12 hours before consuming, but . . . Store the bread wrapped in a cotton cloth inside an earthenware crock or a wicker container or some such suitable receptacle which is not sealed tight.

UTENSILS AND EQUIPMENT

Don't begin baking unless you have the basic tools. The most important are a medium-sized bowl, a wooden spoon, a cup, one flat baking sheet, an oven, a cloth and a sharp knife or razor. With these few tools, you can make an untinned loaf, rising it upside down in the cleaned and floured bowl. After rising, turn it out onto the baking sheet, slash with the knife or razor blade, and bake.

If you want the dough to be tinned, you can buy black tins from hardware stores, health food shops and most cookware suppliers. How many you buy depends on how many you want to cook for . . . or how obsessed you are with bread. Cooking for one means buying smaller tins, but always two — one loaf to eat and one to share. Then you won't be cooking for one for long! I have a range of these heavy tins from the smallest to the largest. Most of the recipes for basic breads are for 1-1.5 kilo loaves. An appropriate tin is 10 cm high, 12 cm wide at the top, 9 cm wide at the bottom and 25 cm long. Or, the dough can be halved to form two loaves in smaller tins 15 cm long, 9 cm high, 8 cm at the base and 9 cm at the top. I also have oval tins which are suitable for small loaves. Good tins can be bought at auctions and in odd places like bakery disposal sales. Metal shapes and tins should be cleaned with soap, well rinsed and dried, oiled thoroughly, and 'burnt in' once. Simply put the empty tin in the oven while baking another loaf. Terracotta shapes can also be used; these are sometimes available glazed. If unglazed, oil the inside and outside thoroughly, bake empty two or three times and re-oil before using. Terracotta flower pots make good bread 'tins'.

Tins can be oiled with a cheap, non-refined oil. Supermarkets usually stock a reasonably sound Spanish olive oil. Use quality oil, if you wish. I use the cheapest of the best, but never the odourless, tasteless and colourless lubricant-style oils. Left-over deep-frying oil which has been preserved with an Umeboshi plum (see Glossary) is a good standby. If I have nothing else available, virgin olive oil makes a magnificent crust when used on the tin! Use a brush to oil tins and trays, a small paint brush is ideal. Wash it well in soapy water and dry before first use.

If you wish to make round loaves, this can be done in a round or oval tin with lower sides than the usual tins, or use a pie tin. Alternatively, the bread can be risen upside down, in a floured wooden bowl like a salad bowl, or a basket lined with floured cotton cloth (e.g. canvas or cheesecloth). For more information, see page 59. The loaf is then turned out for baking. Baskets and canvas are available in some cookware shops. Be sure the bowl or cloth is dredged thoroughly with flour. A round loaf needs to be turned out onto a baking sheet for baking. The removable base of a quiche or flan tin is ideal. Simply brush it with oil. Canvas or cotton cloth can also be used for rising bread sticks or various elongated shapes. Place the cloth with a fold between rolling pins or bottles or breadboards. The stick rises in the fold and is turned out gently onto a baking tray, see page 66.

Bread with a delicate crust and good volume can be made if it is baked under a bowl on the baking sheet. This creates a steamy atmosphere and simulates a baker's oven. Make sure you use an ovenproof bowl which will fit into your oven and which will also cover your loaf adequately. Also ensure you have a baking sheet large enough for the loaf and the bowl. Remove the bowl for the last half of the baking time to allow the crust to develop texture and colour. Leave it on till the last 5 minutes of baking if you don't want crusty bread.

After baking, the bread needs to rest on a raised wire rack or tray so it can cool adequately. The crust will become soggy if left in the tin too long or if rested on a solid base. Wire cake racks are available from department stores or cookware shops, hardware or 'op' shops.

Bowls used for mixing need to be of high quality. Wood, stainless steel, earthenware, crockery or glass are the best materials to use. You will need a range of bowls from the very small for liquifying yeast, to very large for mixing and kneading.

Mixing utensils are important. Wooden spoons are ideal. Dough will be broken up too much if mixed with a metal spoon. Do not buy thin wooden spoons; make sure they have good strong handles or they will break. A wire whisk is invaluable for blending flours or making batters without lumps. A wooden rolling pin is a necessity for certain techniques. Spatulas are essential for transferring dough and leavens smoothly.

The text often specifies to cover a dough with a cloth. This is to exclude most of the air; otherwise a crust will form, spoiling the dough and the final product. It's important to keep the cloth damp. Unprinted cotton cloth is ideal. I use cotton tea-towels or a tablecloth much to my wife's disgust. Old cotton sheets have saved our tea-towel collection. Alternatively, you can enclose the bowl and the dough inside a large plastic bag and seal it.

For measuring, you will need scales which measure up to 2 kilos or more, and scales which have detail down to 5 gm. Small and large measuring jugs for liquids are important. Measuring spoons are necessary for accuracy. Other equipment you will find useful are a mortar and pestle for grinding spices, nuts and seeds; you may prefer to use a vitamiser or coffee grinder. Also a grater for fresh citrus peel and ginger.

Measurements

The only problem I foresee with measurements in this book is with the small weights such as 5 to 15 gm, which refer to yeast and salt. They require an accurate gram scale and commonly available household scales do not measure to this degree. A tablespoon or teaspoon can be substituted for salt or dried yeast, but obviously not for compressed yeast.

15 grams, which is often specified for salt, is a slightly heaped US tablespoon, or a $^1/2$oz. The Imperial tablespoon is a little less than the US tablespoon. The tablespoons and cups I use are to US measures. For those of you who need to compare metric and Imperial for peace of mind, the following equivalents are useful:

$^1/2$ oz = 15 gm = 1 US tablespoon = 1 scant Imperial tablespoon
1 oz = 30 gm
8 oz/$^1/2$ lb = 225 gm
16 oz/1 lb = 450 gm
$35^1/2$ oz/2.2 lb = 1 kilo
1 cup flour = $5^1/2$ ozs or 150 gm
1 cup liquid = 225 millilitres (less than a $^1/4$ litre)
1 pint = 550 ml (a little over $^1/2$ litre)
1 litre = a little over $1^3/4$ pints

THE LOAF OF BREAD

Without reference to quantities, weights and measures, we should explore the beginning and end of making a loaf of bread; once the techniques and methods make sense to you, it should be an easy step to transpose any measurements. If you wish to make twice as much bread as is specified in the recipe, simply double the ingredients. Reducing yeast and salt, for example, is only necessary when much larger quantities (10 kilos and over) are involved.

Yeasted Bread
Mixing
Begin by assembling all your utensils: scales, mixing bowl, small measuring bowl, measuring jug, bread tins, oil, brush, cotton cloths, wooden spoons, measuring spoons, spatula and whisk, flour, salt and yeast. Ensure that you have plenty of room to spread out your equipment and in which to knead. Measure out the flour and salt in a large mixing bowl, more than large enough for the quantity of dough to be made. Too small a bowl is awkward to mix in. Thoroughly mix the flour and salt. If using a mixture of flours, blend well with a wire whisk.

Measure the required quantity of yeast, place it in a small bowl and cream with a little of the measured lukewarm water. Mix this evenly into the flour. Mix the remaining water into the flour, salt and yeast with a wooden spoon. If the recipe calls for 3 cups of water, initially mix in 2 cups and then slowly add as much as is needed of the remaining cup. Flours, wholemeal in particular, absorb different amounts of water. If 3 cups of water suits the flour I have used, it might be $2^3/4$ with yours, or even $3^1/4$. There is also some tolerance in a dough for the amount of liquid added. Some doughs will still work well if a little wetter or drier than I have specified.

When the dough begins to form clusters and come away from the bowl, mix with your hands until smooth and pliable. This dough should not be too sticky. If placed on the table it should show a little adherence. Some bread doughs destined for a tin are sticky on first mixing, but the stickiness decreases as the dough is kneaded. Others intended for crusty loaves which will be baked without a tin need to be quite firm and not adhere to the mixing surface at all.

Kneading
This should be done rhythmically, and not with the violence often associated with it. The object of kneading is to mix the ingredients and produce a suitable dough texture by activating the gluten content of the flour to produce fine strands which are the strength of the dough. Wholemeal wheat flour possesses less gluten because of the large amounts of bran and germ present compared with an equivalent amount of white flour. Therefore, knead it least, but still knead it thoroughly, for 2 to 3 minutes. Soft flours, such as Lowans 80 per

cent Cake Flour also require a short kneading, 2 to 3 minutes. Unbleached white flour can profitably be kneaded for a good 5 minutes.

A good kneading surface should be below your waist height or the exercise becomes uncomfortable and tiring. Flour the surface lightly, never use too much flour at this stage. By kneading, we create cohesion in a dough. Always keep this in mind and centre, don't separate the dough. Face your mixed dough and flatten it a little. Bring the furthest edge towards you and fold on top of the dough to the edge closest. With the heel of your palm, push the top flap away from you into the bottom flap. This creates an elongated shape. Turn it so the narrowest borders are closest and furthest from you, and lift the outer edge over onto the half of the dough closest to you. Repeat the rolling motion. By this method, the outer edges are always brought towards the centre, and the dough acquires structural integrity because of this centring.

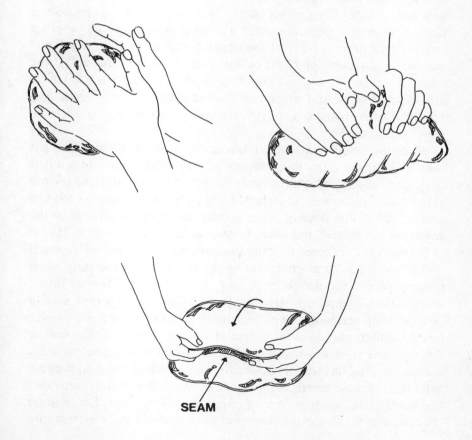

SEAM

After a few minutes of kneading, the dough will, or should, cease to be sticky, and become smooth and pliable. It must not exhibit cracks or be resistant, as both of these indicate a dough which is too dry. If it is too dry knead in more water by placing a tablespoon at a time into a well at the centre of the dough. As stated, a dough to be risen without a tin needs to be a little stiffer or less soft than a tinned dough. If adding more flour, mix thoroughly or the bread will have dry spots.

The analogies surrounding the correct texture of a dough flow freely. Perhaps a good description is 'earlobe' consistency. All very well if you have large fleshy earlobes — a sign of wisdom, strength and longevity — but modern man's are getting smaller. The first good-textured dough you make will be a milestone which you will never forget.

Proving One

Fold the dough so that any seams are on the bottom, place in a floured or oiled bowl which allows plenty of room for expansion — perhaps as much as a doubling of volume — and cover with a damp cotton cloth. It is most important to keep a proving dough covered, whether proving in a tin or a bowl. If the dough forms a dry skin, it will not recover good volume on rising or attain clear crumb in the loaf. If the dough has been proving in an uncovered tin, it will form a skin which lifts during baking and which cracks or wrinkles in the finished loaf. This will often happen also, if the bread is proved in too warm or moist an atmosphere.

When the dough has doubled in volume, punch it down or knock it back by giving it a few firm, but not violent slaps. Roll it into a ball once more and knead it thoroughly for 1 minute. Recheck the texture at this stage; it can still be corrected. If you think the dough is too wet or dry, add a little flour or water to suit. Re-knead briefly, place the seams on the bottom and allow to rise again.

If the loaf is designed for only one proving (rising period), form it into a loaf shape. It is important to shape the dough correctly when tinning. Mould the dough by folding it over on itself several times, stretching and blending after each fold. Again, the moulding should be a centring action designed to achieve a smooth and even interior texture, and to maximise the potential volume of the loaf. Do not use flour on the surface when moulding a loaf as it will prevent joins coalescing. The final action before tinning is rolling the dough into a cylinder, the same length as the tin. Use enough dough to fill only half the depth of the tin. It *must* have only one joining seam. This join on the dough should be on the bottom of the tin, with a smooth even sur-

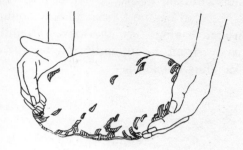

face on top, ready to billow up. Cover with a damp cotton cloth or en-
case in a large plastic bag and leave to rise. When the dough has risen
to the top of the tin, it is baking time.

An active dough made from unbleached white flour or from a mixture containing a large proportion of it, will sometimes rise a little
over the lip of the tin. This forms a characteristic shape as it domes
when baked. Doughs with a larger proportion of wholemeal flour do
not usually do this. So, the few minutes of over-rising to get a slight
'mushrooming' on a white loaf is wasted on yeasted wholemeals
which usually form a wrinkled and unattractive top when over-risen.

Generally, a yeasted loaf should be baked as the loaf reaches the
top of the tin. This is presuming that an appropriate volume of dough
has been placed in the tin. An overful tin causes problems as the
dough will billow uncontrollably and may even flop over if it is too
wet or has been left in the tin too long. A loaf which has not been left
to rise enough in the tin (which is under proved in the tin) will leap up
and probably burst open.

Proving Two
If the dough has to go through another one or two proving periods,
merely repeat the rising and re-shaping procedure and, when baking
time comes, tin the loaf as explained, rise and bake. Proving can go on
too long and the yeast can become exhausted. This is indicated if the
dough sags badly and forms a greyish crust, smelling sour. The
solution here is to add more flour and water and create a new dough
which can be tinned immediately, proved and baked.

Baking
When baking time arrives, make sure the oven is pre-heated to the
specified temperature, or if you have a wood-fired oven, as I do, make
sure it is hot — I insert my hand to measure the temperature. It
should be hot enough for the hand to be left in for 2 to 3 seconds

before being withdrawn. Bake in the top half of the oven or the middle. Refer to the notes on baking times and temperatures (see page 49). Halfway through baking, turn the loaves around so they are evenly baked. Remove from the tin and firmly tap the base. It must give a hollow resounding tone.

Additional Ingredients

There are various other ingredients which we could have used in this theoretical loaf of bread. Oil could be incorporated after the first rising in a loaf with one rising period and after the last rising in a longer maturing dough with several punch downs (or knock backs or punch backs or knock downs), such as Scotch-bake bread (Recipe 35). For a quick rise dough which is mixed, risen once in the tin and baked, add the oil by blending or vitamising with the water to form an emulsion which can be added in place of the water.

Soymilk or cow's milk is mixed with the water and added. Tofu or soya bean curd must be pureed. It can then be rubbed into the flour or simply added before the water. Dry malt is added to the flour. Dark liquid malt can be rubbed into the flour or more conveniently, dissolved into the water. Wheat sprouts and whole cooked cereals, such as unpearled barley or brown rice, are mixed into the dough with the water. It is best to mix them briefly with a little of the water to ensure the grains do not stick together. The slightly milky liquid is good for the dough texture. Wheat sprouts may need to be pulled apart.

The bread can be coated with sesame seeds or wheatmeal by rolling the dough in either just before tinning. Simply spread the seeds or meal on the table and roll. This gives a superb thick coat which is delicious in the crust.

Leaven Risen Bread

The first steps are essentially the same as for yeasted bread. Assemble the utensils and ingredients. Instead of yeast, you will be using liquid leaven. Make sure the leaven is at room temperature. The use of leaven, of course, reduces the amount of extra water to be added. Because leavens may vary in consistency, i.e. in the amount of water they contain, this will affect the amount of water to be added besides the leaven to form a dough. So, use your judgement. If a texture does not feel right, add more water or flour to suit.

Mix the flour(s) and salt thoroughly, stir in the measured quantity of leaven and distribute through the flour with a wooden spoon. Add the required amount of water and mix well. Finish bringing the dough together with your hands and knead till smooth. It is very important that leaven-based bread dough, especially wholemeal wheat, is not too dry. Neither should it stick to the table. Form into a loaf as with yeasted bread. Fill between one-half and two-thirds of the tin. Place in the tin seam down. Cover with a damp cotton cloth and leave to rise. When the dough reaches the top of the tin, bake at the recommended temperature for one hour; smaller loaves take 45 minutes. The easiest bread to make!

Cob

Cob, Coburg, Continental

Exploring and discovering the technique of baking without a tin or enclosing shape is as rewarding as one's first steps into bread baking. Strictly speaking, a Cob loaf is one which is high, round and not slashed, and a Coburg is a slashed or broken cob. In Australia, any loaf which is not tinned is called a Continental; it is probably oval or elongated, not quite white and sometimes slashed . . . according to my panel of seven independent Australians. All bread of this style is best made with a soft or medium soft flour. This does not mean that it cannot be made with strong flour but the results from soft flour are more authentic and more flavoursome.

My panel of Australians agreed unanimously that the Continental loaf is not quite white, which again is more authentic because white flour in Europe is rarely bleached. Lowan's 80 per cent Cake Flour is good for this type of bread, as is their unbleached white. The pastry flour marketed by Salce Bros in Melbourne was made for the job. The best crust comes from a wood-fired oven: gas is more practical for most however and does a good job.

The technique does not require a special recipe. Any of the recipes in this book will work with this method, except those which require a soft or slightly wet dough. Generally, when adapting a recipe for use without a tin, reduce the water content slightly, so as to produce a firmer dough. This is especially necessary with leaven risen breads which tend to go softer or more sticky as they prove. Using larger quantities of leaven makes the dough softer or more liquid in a short period of time, which makes tinning necessary. By adding more leaven, we bring the dough to maturity faster, because the leaven itself is highly mature.

Follow the instructions for the recipe you have chosen, but instead of placing the dough in a tin for proving, mould it into a round shape with any seams on the bottom. Invert the dough and place it in a heavily floured wooden bowl with the seam facing up. A wicker basket or ceramic bowl will be suitable if you cover the bottom with a cotton cloth, heavily dredged with flour. After inverting the dough before baking, peel off the cloth to reveal its weaving imprint on the floured surface. Make sure the bowl used is big enough for the rise and, above all, make sure the bowl is heavily floured so the dough does not stick. Wood is the best surface; dough rarely sticks to it if well floured. Cover the dough with a damp cotton cloth and leave to rise.

The dough's volume should increase by two-thirds. This is less than the usual doubling in bulk. This loaf should be under proved (have a reduced final rising) because it will be slashed. Because the dough is not fully matured, it undergoes quick simulated maturity and springs open and expands when placed in the oven. Slashing the loaf enables this expansion to be confined to the cuts. These burst open to reveal rich colours and textures unique among today's sad commercial imitations.

After proving, carefully invert the wooden bowl onto a baking sheet. Place the baking sheet over the bowl or on the dough before inverting it. This reduces the shock of turning it out.

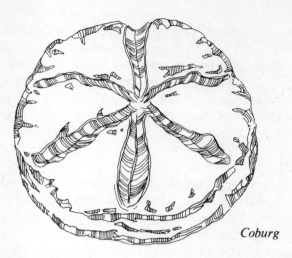

Coburg

The dough should come out onto the tray heavily dredged with flour and nicely shaped. Immediately, slash the loaf 2 to 3 cm deep in a cross, double cross, crescent slit or chequerboard; whichever shape appeals. Use a very sharp implement, a barber's razor or a new razor blade. The cut must be decisive. The more this loaf is handled, the more likely it is not to recover its volume. Bake immediately at the specified temperature for leaven, high in the oven. The slash should open out as the loaf responds to the initial heat. After 15 to 20 minutes, remove the baking sheet, and let the loaf sit on the oven racks for the remaining baking time. This results in a well baked base. Wholemeal requires 5 to 10 minutes more baking than white flour bread. Remove the loaf and place on a wire rack to cool. This loaf is a delight — superbly coloured and textured, with an enveloping delicious crust, resembling an exotic Mars-scape — bread with character.

Round loaves can be risen in a round tin. These can be slashed 10 minutes after being placed in the tin. The cuts open and grow, being well developed by baking time. Alternatively, underprove and slash immediately before baking. When making any type of bread which is to be slashed, the dough must *not* be too wet or slack or it will spread uncontrollably or the slash will not open satisfactorily.

A Cob in English terminology is a round loaf which is not slashed. It differs from the slashed Coburg or crusty Continental loaf in that the dough for a Cob, like tinned bread, should fully double its bulk in the final proving or rising period. This is because it will be less likely to burst open in the oven, as all of its expanding will be done. A baker's trick is to prick the dough with a sharp skewer or with nails set in a cluster (called docking). This allows any excess gas to escape, the loaf does not usually burst open and the characteristic smooth, round shape is maintained. This should be made with a stiff dough compared to the softer or slacker tinned bread dough. The Cob can be risen in a round tin, an inverted bowl or a basket, like the Coburg or Continental, or can be left free-standing. Be sure to mould the shape well so that it grows without splitting. A Cob will burst open if placed in too hot an oven.

Under a Bowl

By baking a round loaf of bread under an earthenware bowl you can obtain a sensational crust and good volume. Make sure the bowl is big enough to contain the loaf and that it will fit into your oven. When you tip the bread out of the rising bowl onto a baking sheet, simply place the baking bowl over the dough and slip the lot into the oven. You can use the same bowl for rising and baking provided it is cleaned first. This creates a steamy atmosphere and a paper-thin 'eggshell' crust. Generally, remove the bowl after 40 minutes of baking for leaven bread and allow the crust to brown for 5 to 10 minutes, to whatever degree you choose. For yeast bread, remove the bowl after 20 minutes.

In order to give you a guide to quantities for Cobs, Coburgs and Continentals which can, as mentioned, be made from most doughs in this book, I have included the following recipes. The dough may appear as though it won't come together, but work at it.

Quantities for Cob, Coburg or Continental loaves, either leaven risen or yeasted, are remarkably easy to calculate. I was surprised to see the barm Cob loaf is of greater volume than the yeasted one. The crusts of all three are quite individual, with the leaven loaf having the most 'exotic' colours.

1 Yeasted

500 gm unbleached white flour
10 gm salt
10 gm yeast
1 1/4 cups warm water

Mix the dough as described and leave for a first rising of 1 1/2 hours.

Knead well, shape into a high sphere so it will maintain its roundness during the final proving of 3/4 hour for a Coburg and 1 hour for a Cob. Slash the Coburg and bake at 220°C (425°F) for 35 minutes, moving to a lower rack if the crust burns, or turning the oven down to 205°C (400°F).

Prick the Cob to a depth of 6 cm, in a circle, about seven times with a wooden skewer. If this appears to deflate the dough slightly, don't panic, as you can leave the dough 5 minutes to recover any lost volume. Bake as for the Coburg.

2 Leaven or Barm Risen

500 gm unbleached white flour
5 gm salt
1 cup barm or leaven
$^3/_4$ cup warm water

First rising $^1/_2$-$^3/_4$ hour: by this time the dough will have just activated. Form into a free standing sphere, cover and rise 2$^1/_2$ hours for barm and 2 to 2$^1/_2$ hours for leaven; or rise in an inverted bowl for a similar period. Bake for 45 minutes at 215°C (415°F) for barm and 205°C (400°F) for leaven.

Vienna
See Recipe 10.

Plaited
See Recipe 59. An attractive shape results from tinning a plaited loaf. The surface has the attractive plaits while the bulk of the bread is a convenient square.

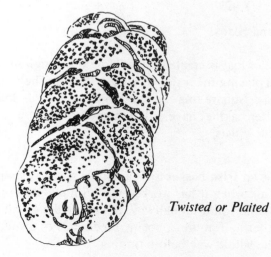

Twisted or Plaited

Cottage

Cottage loaf

The cottage loaf can be difficult, but a successful one is a delight. A stiff dough is required. After first proving, divide 1 kilo of dough into two portions of 600 gm and 400 gm. Form each into a ball and allow them to prove, covering well, so a skin does not form. After 45 minutes, the dough should be three-quarters proved. Slash a 4 cm (1$^1/_2$ inch) wide cross at the centre of the larger dough which will form the bottom of the loaf. Lift the smaller portion onto the top of the bigger one with a slide. It should cover the cuts. Gently poke a hole 4 cm (1$^1/_2$ inches) deep into the centre of the top dough with your thumb. Allow 5 minutes for it to recover from this 'bashing'. Bake. If the 'cottage' collapses, it is probably because your dough was too soft or slack, or because it was over-proved, i.e. had been allowed to rise too long. Try again!

Shapes and Sizes

Split Tin

This type of loaf is created by dividing the dough into two equal portions and placing them side by side in the tin. They grow together and 'kiss'. Large square tins can contain up to a dozen loaves side by side which, after baking, have only top and bottom crusts, some with one or two side crusts.

Spirals

Known as an Irish basket loaf, a double spiral is simple to shape and exhilarating when it has worked well. Simply shape the dough into a long oval and roll it up halfway. Stand the dough on its base and roll up the other half in the opposite direction. For a single spiral, simply roll up the whole way before tinning.

Spiral loaf

Rolls and Muffins

Usually I make rolls with a yeasted dough and muffins with a leaven dough. This is because leaven doughs take longer to rise and the free-standing dough tends to spread as it becomes more slack. A gem scone iron is an ideal implement for baking leaven muffins. These are made from cast iron and are about 15 cm x 30 cm (6 x 12 inches) with 12 cups.

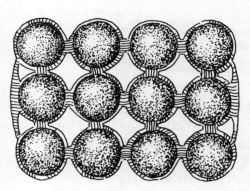

Rolls or muffins can be made with any of the yeast or leaven doughs described in the preceding pages. Use 750 gm flour and this will make twelve 100 gm rolls or muffins or ten 120 gm ones. I can recommend the Scotch-bake dough (Recipe 35) for the finest rolls. Using soymilk exclusively as the liquid in the dough makes soft light rolls.

When you have made up the dough and it has proved once, separate and weigh out the required amounts. Shape the rolls into high domes with seams on the bottom. This allows for just a little spreading. Place them on an oiled baking sheet, cover and allow 15 minutes to rise or until doubled in size. Bake at the same temperature as bread for 15 to 20 minutes. Don't be afraid to put the rolls too close together on the baking sheet as then they will 'kiss' allowing you the pleasure of breaking them apart and revealing the delicate honeycomb inside.

Shape muffins into a smooth ball and place them in the oiled gem scone iron or whatever cupped cake tray you have. They need to be risen for 3 to 4 hours or until twice the original bulk. Bake as for rolls.

Rolls and muffins can be glazed with innumerable concoctions:

  (1) An egg with its volume of water, beaten well
  (2) The above with 1 teaspoon of natural soy sauce (shoyu*)
  (3) 1 cup water mixed with 1 tablespoon shoyu
  (4) Soymilk
  (5) Water
  (6) Malt extract dissolved in water
  (7) Soymilk and honey (for sweet rolls and muffins)
  (8) Maple syrup (see Brioche, Recipe 44)

They can also be rolled in sesame, sunflower or poppy seeds.

Bread Sticks

French stick

(a) Yeasted

Scotch-bake dough is especially good for making bread sticks. You could consider making sticks and rolls with the remaining half of your dough, see page 92. Apart from that, use any of the yeasted dough recipes in this book. The only restriction on making sticks is the size of your oven. Unfortunately, most home made sticks can't be as long as the impressive sticks from a proper baker's oven.

Divide 1 kilo of dough into three equal proportions. Shape each into a 'cigar' and use a rolling pin to roll it into an elongated oval 1 cm (1/4 inch) thick. Brush the long edge, away from you, with a little water and roll up the dough tightly. Place it seam down on an oiled baking sheet. Cover and allow to rise for 15 to 20 minutes or until it doubles in bulk. Slash the dough with diagonal cuts. Brush with water for a crisper crust. Bake at 220°C (425°F) for 15 to 20 minutes.

* See *Natural Tucker*, page 8.

(b) Leaven risen

Bread sticks based on a leaven need an enclosing shape to prevent them wandering all over the baking sheet. Special baskets and tins are available from some cookery stores. These need to be lined with a heavily floured cotton cloth. Use any of the leaven based doughs. Recipe 4 is excellent. Place the dough, formed into a shape similar to the basket, onto the floured cloth in the basket. Cover with a damp cotton cloth and leave for 3 to 4 hours to increase in size by two-thirds. Alternatively, place a floured canvas or cotton cloth between rolling pins, bottles or other supports. The stick can rise in this and be turned out in a similar manner. Turn out onto an oiled baking sheet by lifting the cloth and rolling the dough onto the tray. Slash the surface of the dough diagonally several times. Bake at 205°C (400°F) for 35 minutes.

PART TWO

RECIPES

This is the place in which I absolve myself of all responsibility for your mistakes. Please read The Loaf of Bread, pages 53-9, before proceeding with the recipes. In fact, all the information in Part 1 will help you.

The directions in many of the recipes are brief, but there are key recipes which contain full directions. These will be referred to in the recipes in which methods are not outlined, but which are the same as the key recipes. The appropriate page reference is given with each recipe.

This chart indicates how many loaves you can plan for, depending on the quantity of flour used.

Flour	No of Loaves
550 gm	1 medium (750 gm)
750 gm	1 large (1.2 to 1.4 kilo) or 2 small (500 gm)
1 kilo	2 medium, 3 small or 1 very large
1.5 kilos	2 large, 3 medium or 4 small

Following is a guide to the flour-water ratio of doughs. It is approximate because some doughs need to be softer or more liquid than others, and therefore require a little more water. For example, a dough using 500 gm of unbleached white flour requires $1^1/_4$ cups of water for a Cob or free-standing round loaf, and $1^1/_2$ cups for a tinned egg bread.

	Unbleached white	Eighty per cent	Wholemeal
500 gm	$1^1/_4$ cups water	$1^1/_4$	$1^1/_3$-$1^1/_2$
750 gm	$1^2/_3$	2	$2^1/_4$-$2^1/_2$
1 kilo	2 (plus a little more)	$2^1/_4$	$2^3/_4$

When using wholemeal flour, remember that the quantity of water required can vary up to half a cup (see page 24). Ovens vary notoriously so, unless you are familiar with baking bread in your particular oven, be prepared for a few adjustments. Baking can be a risky undertaking! Good luck!

BASIC LEAVEN BREADS

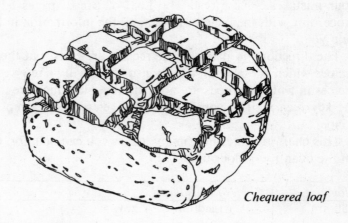

Chequered loaf

1   One hundred per cent wholemeal — feed the man wheat!

750 gm wholemeal wheat flour
¹/2 teaspoon salt
2 cups leaven
1¹/4 cups water

Mix flour and salt in a bowl big enough to allow for vigorous mixing.
A bigger bowl is better than a smaller one. Mix in the leaven, and
evenly distribute with a wooden spoon. Add the water in stages until a
smooth, pliable dough is formed. Add more or less water as necessary,
depending on the absorption rate of the flour. Knead well for 2
minutes. Cut the dough in half if making two loaves and place in tins.
The dough should two-thirds fill the tin. Ensure the upper surface of
the dough is smooth with no seams or cracks. The joining seam from
moulding should be placed on the bottom, allowing the dough to
billow upwards with a smooth surface. Cover with a damp cotton
cloth (tea-towel) and allow 4 to 5 hours to rise in summer, 5 to 7
hours in winter. A good winter warm spot can reduce this to 5 hours.
At any rate, the dough should reach the top of the tin. Bake in the top

half or the middle of the oven at 205°C (400°F). This temperature can be raised to 220°C (425°F) if you turn the oven down to 200°C (400°F) for the last half hour of baking. In the former case the bread should take 1 hour, in the latter 50 minutes. Untin the loaves and place in the oven upside-down for a further 5 minutes if you like a crust.

Sesame-wheat When the loaves have been formed, spread a large amount of sesame seeds on the table, and roll the loaf in them. If the dough is a little dry or floury, moisten it with water on the outside. This results in a delicious encrustation.

2 Eighty per cent wholemeal wheat

Eighty per cent flour is available in Australia from Lowan Whole-foods, called Cake Flour. As such it is a soft flour, and bread made from it does not keep as well as that made from hard wheat. This is more than compensated for by the fact that it is good bread with an excellent crust. Salce Bros Fine Flour is another flour of similar extraction to Lowan's flour. It is probably the best of its type in Australia. Approximately 80 per cent flour can be made by sifting 100 per cent wholemeal flour (see page 28). Give it at least 3 hours to cool and eat it within 1 day. Rising the dough in a bowl is a very sucessful technique with this flour.

> *550 gm 80 per cent wheat flour*
> *$^1/_2$ teaspoon salt*
> *1 cup leaven (made with 80 per cent flour)*
> *1 cup water*

Follow the directions for Recipe 1, or rise in a bowl (see pages 59-61).

3 Fifty per cent wholemeal wheat

Lighter than 100 per cent but still flavoursome.

> *350 gm wholemeal wheat flour*
> *350 gm unbleached white flour*
> *$^1/_2$ teaspoon salt*
> *2 cups leaven*
> *$1^1/_4$-$1^1/_3$ cups water*

Thoroughly mix the flours and proceed according to Recipe 1.

4 Not quite white

This bread definitely benefits from rising in a bowl to make a round Continental or French style loaf. The crust is very good. If possible leave for 4 hours to cool. Lowans Unbleached Bread Flour is excellent for this recipe.

> *550 gm unbleached white flour*
> *$^1/_2$ teaspoon salt*
> *1 cup wholemeal or white leaven (wholemeal gives the best flavour)*
> *1-1$^1/_5$ cups water*

Knead the dough well, more than for wholemeal. Place in a bowl, cover and allow 1 hour to prove. Then reshape it and place in an oiled tin two-thirds full or in a floured wooden bowl. When the dough reaches the top of the tin, bake at 220°C (425°F) for 45 minutes. For the bowl, when the dough has increased in volume by one-third, turn out, slash and bake. The oven 'kick' is as high as a yeasted loaf.

5 Quality quickly

If a free-form loaf is made from a larger quantity of leaven than usual, it can be proved for just 1 hour, slashed and baked. By adding more leaven, we can bring the dough to maturity faster, because the leaven itself is highly mature. When mixed with raw flour, which is immature because it has undergone no fermentation, the dough gains instant maturity. So, after 1 hour, the loaf has settled enough for baking.

> *250 gm wholemeal wheat flour*
> *300 gm unbleached white flour*
> *$^1/_2$ teaspoon salt*
> *2 cups leaven*
> *$^1/_2$ cup water*

Thoroughly mix the flours and follow the directions for Recipe 1. Form the loaf into a high round. Cover and prove for 1 hour. Slash and bake at 205°C (400°F) for 45 minutes.

6 No need to knead (i)

This recipe is designed for those of you who, for various reasons, cannot do much kneading. It is better to knead a dough, even wholemeal, because the loaf has more integrity. However no knead is better than no bread.

550 gm wholemeal wheat flour
¹/₂ teaspoon salt
1 cup leaven
1 cup plus one tablespoon warm water

Dissolve the salt in a little water and add to the flour. Stir in the leaven until well distributed. Add the water, and mix the dough with your hands. It should be smooth, not sticky. Form it into a loaf and place in an oiled tin. Allow 4 to 6 hours to at least double in bulk. Bake at 205°C (400°F) for 55 minutes. Untin and return to the oven for 5 minutes.

7   Wheat sprout bread

A sweet wheaty experience. Because of the malt sugars in the sprouts, a delicious crust forms on this bread. Wheat sprouts can be included in any of the previous recipes. These quantities are for three medium sized loaves. Reduce them, using Recipe 1 as a guide for quantities if you choose. Three loaves probably aren't enough!

1.5 kilos wholemeal wheat flour
300 gm wheat sprouts 5 to 6 days old, see page 44.
   (This can be increased if you can cope with it. Separate
   the wheat sprouts if they are very intertwined.)
1¹/₂ teaspoons salt
3 cups leaven
2¹/₂ cups water

Proceed as for Recipe 1 adding the sprouts with the water.

8   Wholemeal and wholegrain

Whole cereal grains can add moisture and flavour to a loaf whether it is made from 100 per cent or less flour. Cooked brown rice is perhaps the best grain to add to wheat bread. Cooked whole buckwheat, hulled millet and barley are the most suitable grains to use besides rice. These cereals are cooked in the same way as rice. Break up the grains to avoid lumps in the bread.

750 gm wholemeal wheat flour
¹/₂ teaspoon salt
2 cups leaven
200 gm cooked brown rice
1¹/₄ cups water

Follow the directions for Recipe 1. Break up the grains in the water and add with it. Wholegrains can be incorporated in any of the previous recipes; simply use an equivalent amount.

9   Soya wheat bread (i)

The addition of tofu makes this into a full flavoured loaf with an excellent protein rating. This loaf has more volume than its yeasted
counterpart (Recipe 31) and keeps extremely well.

> *500 gm wholemeal wheat flour*
> *1 teaspoon salt*
> *1 cup leaven*
> *¹/2 cup water*
> *150 gm tofu, pureed*

Follow the directions for Recipe 1. Add the tofu with the water.

10   Soy-Vienna or the Orient Express

Totally unorthodox but totally delicious.

> *400 gm unbleached white flour*
> *150 gm 80 per cent wheat flour*
> *1 teaspoon salt*
> *³/4 cup wholemeal leaven or barm*
> *¹/2 teaspoon liquid malt extract*
> *¹/2 teaspoon honey*
> *³/4 cup soymilk and ¹/2 cup water mixed*
> *1¹/2 teaspoons unrefined oil (this should not be strongly*
> *   flavoured)*

Mix flours and salt thoroughly. Stir in the leaven until evenly distributed. Dissolve the malt and honey in the milk-water mixture and add
to the dough along with the oil. Mix with a wooden spoon until the
dough comes together and then knead until a smooth, slightly stiff
dough is formed. Place in an air-tight container and refrigerate overnight or for 8 hours. Re-knead briefly, place in a bowl, cover and
allow to warm up for 1 hour. Re-shape and place in a heavily floured
cloth set between two bottles or a similar enclosing space. The shape
you are aiming for is the conventional elongated oval. After 1 to 2
hours the dough should be sufficiently active for you to roll it onto an
oiled baking sheet. Slash it, give it a few minutes to recover from
slashing and bake at 205°C (400°F) for 35 to 40 minutes. Refer to The
Loaf of Bread (page 59) for illumination on free-form techniques.

11 A touch of rye (i)

This is a recipe described in my previous book.* I repeat it because it is so good. The mixture responds well to rising in a bowl or elongated shape. If rising in a bowl, use unbleached white flour or rye flour as dusting for an interesting crust colour.

> *250 gm unbleached white flour*
> *250 gm wholemeal wheat flour*
> *250 gm wholemeal rye flour (this can be sifted for a lighter*
> *   bread)*
> *1 teaspoon salt*
> *2 teaspoons caraway seeds (optional)*
> *2 cups leaven*
> *1¹/₃ cups plus 1 tablespoon water*

Thoroughly mix the flours and proceed as for Recipe 1. Add caraway seeds with the salt.

12 A touch of barley

As with Recipe 11, one-third of this bread is non-wheat. Barley flour is marketed by Lowan Wholefoods. The barley flavour is very appetising. If you haven't used barley in bread before you will be an instant convert. The barley should not be too coarsely ground.

> *250 gm unbleached white flour*
> *250 gm wholemeal wheat flour*
> *250 gm barley flour or fine meal*
> *1 teaspoon salt*
> *2 cups leaven*
> *1¹/₂ cups water*

The method is the same as Recipe 1. Thoroughly mix the flours first. Barley flour can be replaced by oat flour or fine oatmeal, buckwheat flour or millet flour, all very good eating. The oatmeal should not be too coarse and must be fresh, see page 30. The millet should be finely ground.

---

* *Natural Tucker*, page 128, the Yugoslavian miller's recipe.

13   Six of one, half a dozen of the other

Instead of using one-third, interesting bread results from using half non-wheat flour. This is most satisfactory if you use rye or barley. You can use either unbleached white, 100 per cent wholemeal or 80 per cent for the wheat half. Unbleached white brings out the flavour of the non-wheat flour more strongly. The liquid quantity varies from $1^1/4$ to $1^1/2$ cups depending on what type of wheat flour is used, with wholemeal requiring the most.

> *400 gm wheat flour*
> *350 gm barley or rye flour*
> *1 teaspoon salt*
> *2 cups wheat leaven*
> *$1^1/4$-$1^1/2$ cups water*

If rye flour is used in this recipe, it can be risen in an oval shaped bowl and turned out. This seems to be a traditional shape for this bread. Thoroughly mix the flours and see Recipe 1 for directions.

14   One hundred per cent rye bread (schwartzbrot)

For those who like it, 100 per cent leaven risen rye bread is delicious, especially with an appropriate companion such as dill pickles or fish. If the rye flour is sifted, removing the coarsest bran, a lighter bread will result. Caraway, dill or cummin seeds complement this bread and make it more digestible.

> *750 gm rye flour*
> *1 teaspoon salt*
> *1-2 teaspoons caraway seeds*
> *3 cups rye leaven*
> *$1^1/4$ cups water*

Mix the salt with the flour and seeds and stir in the leaven and water. This dough is somewhat different to wheat and can be intimidating. It must be slightly sticky and definitely difficult to handle. Add a little water if the dough appears too dry. Knead for 2 to 3 minutes. Form into one large or two smaller loaves. Spread rye flour on the table and roll the loaf in it, making sure the top is well dredged. Place in a tin two-thirds full or rise in a bowl if you wish. Cover with a damp cloth and leave to rise 4 to 5 hours in summer, 5 to 7 hours in winter. Bake at 205°C (400°F) for 1 hour. Untin and bake a further 5 minutes if you like a well developed crust. 100 per cent rye bread needs at least 12 hours to settle after baking. By mixing 1 teaspoon of liquid malt extract into the leaven, an even darker flavoured and coloured loaf results.

15   Rye sprout bread

Rye sprouts are made like wheat sprouts, see page 44. Using them makes rye bread something very special. The sugars in the sprouts promote a better rise and a most attractive appearance, as the interior of the rye sprout becomes translucent. A large quantity of sprouts produces a very difficult loaf to handle, but with excellent flavour and keeping qualities. Break up the tangle of sprouts in the water before adding them to the mixture.

750 gm rye flour
1 teaspoon salt
1-2 teaspoons caraway seeds
3 cups rye leaven
1¼ cups water
300-500 gm rye sprouts

Follow the directions for Recipe 14. Add the sprouts along with the water.

YEASTED BREADS

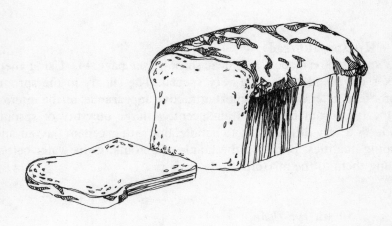

Wholemeal wheat bread is best made with a leaven. The process is easier, the bread rises as much and the texture is not like a pudding as wholemeal breads can tend to be. Further the bread is more digestible because of the extensive action of the leaven in pre-digesting the wheat. However, wholemeal wheat bread can also be made with yeast, and the results are excellent in the right hands.

Breads made on the one-third principle, e.g. one-third oatmeal, one-third wholemeal wheat, one-third unbleached white, are the exception as the flavour of the non-wheat flour seems accentuated by using yeast. Yeast really comes into its own, however, with the higher softer loaves which appeal to modern palates and eyes.

Because of its strong expanding tendency as opposed to leaven, yeast requires a lot more salt. The contracting tendency of the salt balances the opposite quality of the yeast. Salt textures a yeasted bread dough, whereas leaven has this capacity in itself. Saltless yeast bread is insipid and is a less digestible food than that in which a proper measure of salt is employed. Reduce the quantity of salt I have recommended if you like, as it is to my taste.

As mentioned in the section on yeast, I recommend compressed yeast. If you only have dried yeast, substitute as directed on page 46.

16 Wholemeal wheat yeasted bread

Many overseas cookbooks instruct that wholemeal should not be kneaded, or at least only very briefly. I don't know if we have quite different flour in Australia, but my experience is that wholemeal wheat doughs benefit from 2 to 3 minutes good kneading. Unkneaded wholemeal can result in a pudding texture. Granted, doughs made from unbleached white or 80 per cent flour benefit from a longer kneading, but it is still necesssary to knead wholemeal wheat dough. Wholemeal does not respond to long fermentation periods, e.g. 15 hours or more, as well as flours of higher extraction such as 80 per cent or unbleached white.

Remember that the quantities given here for wholemeal wheat are as accurate as possible, taking into consideration the varying capacities of wholemeal wheat flours to absorb water.

750 gm wholemeal wheat flour (preferably organic and stoneground)
15 gm salt
15 gm yeast
2¹/₄ to 2¹/₂ cups lukewarm water

Mix the salt and the flour. Dissolve the yeast in half a cup of the water. Mix the yeast liquid into the flour and add 1¹/₂ cups of water. Incorporate the water into the flour with a wooden spoon and then bring the dough together with your hands. Add more water if necessary to form a smooth, pliable dough. Make sure the dough is not too dry: this is indicated by cracks or lack of pliability. If the dough is too wet, add flour a little at a time until it is manageable. This dough is a little sticky at first, but becomes smooth with kneading. Knead for 2 to 3 minutes. Place the dough in a bowl and cover with a damp cloth. Leave to rise for 2 hours until doubled in bulk. Re-knead the dough briefly and form into a loaf shape with any seams on the bottom. Add a little more water if the dough feels too firm or dry, and knead it in. Don't be intimidated! Place the dough in an oiled tin, cover with a damp cotton cloth (tea-towel) and leave until it doubles in bulk which will take approximately 1 hour in a warm environment. Bake in the centre of a 220°C (425°F) oven for 35 to 45 minutes. Alternatively, bake at 205°C (400°F) for 45 minutes to 1 hour. Untin and place upside down in the oven for 2 to 3 minutes. Cool on a wire rack for at least 1 hour and preferably 6 hours.

17   Half-meal bread

(a)   Short-time dough
500 gm wholemeal wheat flour
500 gm unbleached white flour
25 gm salt
25 gm yeast
3¹/₄ cups water

Mix the flours thoroughly and combine all the ingredients as in Recipe 16. Knead well until a smooth dough is formed. Divide the dough and place in oiled tins or floured bowls to rise. The dough should have doubled in bulk in 2 hours. Bake at 220ºC (425ºF) for 40 minutes. One large loaf, about 1.5 kilos, would take 1 hour. Remove the bread from the tin and bake a further 2 to 3 minutes. Cool well before cutting.

(b)   Longer-time dough
500 gm wholemeal wheat flour
500 gm unbleached white flour
25 gm salt
5 gm yeast
3¹/₄ cups water

Blend the flours well and mix all the ingredients as in Recipe 16. Place in a bowl and cover the dough with a plastic bag or make sure you keep the cotton covering cloth damp. It is a disaster if the proving dough forms a crust, as it never regains its activity properly and will contain lumps. Leave the dough overnight or for 8 hours. By this time, the yeast will have completely activated the dough. Re-knead and leave for a further 2 hours, then knead again and tin the dough. To a point (about 15 hours) the dough will improve with age. Bake as for Recipe 16. This bread tastes superior to short-time doughs and has a smell I had not experienced since childhood. Well matured bread such as this benefits from ¹/₂ teaspoon of liquid malt extract, mixed into the water during the initial stages of mixing.

18   Country bread

Why this is called Country bread I don't know. Time and time again, when I have made it, people have said, 'Oh! Country bread!' Maybe it's the shape — round, slashed and bursting with character. Perhaps city bread seems to them mechanically shaped and mechanically coloured and flavoured.

Country bread is made with 80 per cent wholemeal flour. If you do not have access to this flour, sift 100 per cent wholemeal wheat flour and make it (page 28). If you go on sifting some of the commercial wholemeals available in the supermarkets, you will end up with bleached white flour! It is best to sift stoneground wholemeal. A special flour for this bread is marketed in Melbourne by Salce Bros. They call it pastry flour, which it is, but it also makes unforgettable bread.

750 gm 80 per cent wholemeal wheat flour
15 gm salt
15 gm yeast
2 cups plus 2 tablespoons water

Proceed as for Recipe 16. After the first rising period, place the dough in a heavily floured wooden bowl to rise. When doubled in bulk, turn out onto a baking sheet, slash in a cross or chequerboard formation (see pages 59-61), and bake at 220°C (425°F) for 35 to 45 minutes. After 15 minutes of baking, remove the baking sheet so the bottom will be adequately cooked.

19   No need to knead (ii)

550 gm wholemeal wheat flour
15 gm yeast
15 gm salt
1 tablespoon unrefined oil
1 1/2 cups warm water

Cream the yeast in a little of the water. Dissolve the salt in the remaining water and whisk in the oil. Add the yeast to the flour and stir it in. Pour in the remaining liquid and bring the dough together with your hands, giving it a thorough mix. Add more flour if the mixture is sticky. It should be quite easy to handle. Place in an oiled bread tin, about half full, cover and allow to rise for 1 1/4 hours. Bake at 205°C (400°F) for 40 minutes. Untin and return to the oven for 5 minutes.

20   Not quite white yeasted bread (i)

It's not quite white but only the very observant will spot that. I had not eaten white bread for years until I discovered unbleached white flour. This bread forms only an occasional treat for us. After making it, like us, you will find it hard to believe that all white bread once tasted like it.

> *750 gm unbleached white flour*
> *15 gm salt*
> *1 tablespoon olive oil*
> *15 gm yeast*
> *1 teaspoon liquid malt extract*
> *1²/₃ cups water*

Mix the salt and flour. Dissolve the yeast and malt in a little of the water. Rub the oil into the flour or blend it with the rest of the water. Mix thoroughly through the flour. Add the remaining water and mix into a smooth pliable dough. Place the dough in a bowl big enough to allow plenty of room for expansion, and cover with a damp cotton cloth. Allow 2 hours to rise in a warm place. Re-knead and leave for a further 2 hours to mature. Tin the dough, cover and keep warm (not too warm!). The bread should have doubled in volume and risen to the top of the tin in 1 hour. Bake at 220ºC (425ºF) for 35 to 45 minutes. The loaf will 'kick' 5 to 10 cm in the oven.

This loaf could have been made without the oil or malt, but this results in a less rich bread which stales quickly. 150 gm of cooked brown rices makes it a longer keeper with more flavour.

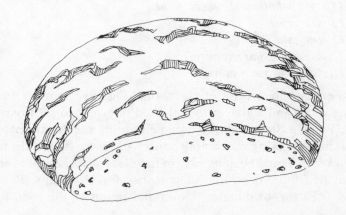

21 Not quite white yeasted bread (ii)

> *500 gm unbleached white flour*
> *500 gm 80 per cent wheat flour*
> *25 gm yeast*
> *25 gm salt*
> *2¹/₂ cups water*

Mix the flours thoroughly. Dissolve the yeast in ¹/₂ cup water and dissolve the salt in the remaining water. Mix the yeast liquid into the flour with a wooden spoon. Add the remaining water. Stir until the dough begins to form. Bring it together with your hands and knead for 2 to 3 minutes until smooth and pliable. Place in a bowl, cover and leave 2 hours to rise in a warm place. Re-knead for 2 minutes, cover and leave to rise for 1¹/₂ hours. Remove from the bowl, knead for 1 minute and mould into two rounds or four ovals about 20.5 cm x 5 cm wide (8 x 2 inches), which will resemble the French baton. Rise in a wooden bowl as described on page 60 or on canvas (see page 67). When the dough is three times its volume, slash the surface. The cuts on the oval loaves must be diagonal or they will not open. The round loaves can be slashed as described on page 61.

Bake at 220°C (425°F) for 40 minutes or 25 minutes for the sticks. If desired, brush or spray the surface of the loaves with water before putting them into the oven, and every 5 minutes for the first 15 minutes. This gives a really good crust.

22 A touch of rye (ii)
This is a well flavoured and satisfying bread.

> *250 gm wholemeal rye flour*
> *250 gm wholemeal wheat flour*
> *250 gm unbleached white flour*
> *2 teaspoons caraway seeds*
> *15 gm salt*
> *15 gm yeast*
> *2¹/₄ cups lukewarm water*
> *1 teaspoon liquid malt extract or pure malt powder (optional)*

Blend the flours well and mix in the seeds. The directions are the same as for Recipe 16 except that the final proving is for 45 minutes. If using the malt, dissolve it in the water with the yeast, and use a little less water.

23 Leaven flavoured, yeast boosted rye bread

Rye does not respond to yeast as well as wheat. The leaven process accentuates the rye flavour and gives the bread a balancing sourness. If a larger proportion of rye than in this recipe is used in yeast bread, I find the bread distinctly lacking in an essential ingredient — the leaven.

> *400 gm wholemeal rye flour*
> *350 gm wheat flour (either 80 per cent, unbleached white or wholemeal)*
> *2 teaspoons caraway seeds*
> *15 gm salt*
> *15 gm yeast*
> *2 cups rye leaven*
> *1³/4 cups water with wholemeal (The quantity of water varies depending on which flour is used.)*
> *1 teaspoon liquid malt extract or pure malt powder (optional)*

The procedure is the same as for Recipe 16. Mix the seeds into the flour. Add the leaven before the water. Roll the loaf in rye flour before tinning. 200 gm of rye sprouts or soaked cooked rye can be added for a hearty loaf.

24 Barely barley

I could wax poetic over the aroma and flavour of this barley touched loaf. There are four variations presented here. I favour the combination of two-thirds unbleached white flour with one-third barley. It's a photo finish with (c), however.

(a) *250 gm barley flour or fine meal*
     250 gm wholemeal wheat flour
     250 gm unbleached white flour
     15 gm salt
     15 gm yeast
     2¹/4 cups water

(b) *250 gm barley flour or fine meal*
     250 gm 80 per cent wheat flour
     250 gm unbleached white flour

The salt, yeast and water quantities are the same as (a).

(c)   *250 gm barley flour or fine meal*
      500 gm 80 per cent wheat flour
The salt, yeast and water quantities are the same as (a).

(d)   *500 gm unbleached white flour*
      250 gm barley flour or fine meal
      2 cups water
The salt and yeast quantities are the same as (a).

Mix the flours thoroughly and then proceed as in Recipe 16.

25 Barley-wheat bread

This is a heavier bread with a stronger barley flavour. Either 100 or 80 per cent or unbleached white wheat flours can be used. The water quantities vary between 2¼ to 2½ cups, more or less, with wholemeal requiring the most. If the dough seems too dry after the first rising, thoroughly knead a little more water into it.

375 gm barley flour or fine meal
375 gm wheat flour (either 80 per cent, unbleached white or wholemeal)
15 gm salt
15 gm yeast
2¼-2⅓ cups water (depending on which flour is used).

Mix the flours thoroughly and follow the directions for Recipe 16.

26 Oat, buckwheat and millet variations

The above flours can be substituted for barley in Recipes 24 and 25. They are especially good in a combination like two-thirds unbleached white flour and one-third non-wheat flour. Millet is exceptional in this combination. Care should be taken that the oatmeal is not too coarsely ground and is fresh (see page 30). Stale oatmeal has an unpleasant bitter flavour. The oatmeal variation can tolerate a soft or sticky dough as water is absorbed during proving. The millet and buckwheat flours should be finely ground as opposed to meal.

27 Corn bread

Serve this with chilli red kidney beans and pot roast vegetables. It is not a high rising bread, and needs to be baked in a 5 cm (2 inch) deep baking tray, approximately 30 cm x 15 cm (12 x 6 inches), or a larger, slightly shallower one. This bread is very attractive risen in a round wooden bowl, and turned out to bake. Dredge the bowl with the same mixture of flour that is employed in the bread. Slash the crust with parallel lines.

> *375 gm 80 per cent wheat flour*
> *375 gm yellow corn meal (polenta). (White maize meal can*
> *be used but is not as well coloured or flavoured.)*
> *20 gm salt*
> *15 gm yeast*
> *1¹/₂ tablespoons unrefined corn oil or olive oil*
> *1³/₄ cups lukewarm water*

The method is the same as for Recipe 16. Rub the oil into the mixed flours.

28 Sesame wheat bread

Sesame paste or tahina can be used in the same manner as oil in a bread dough. Sesame paste is different from tahina. The former is more concentrated and needs to be thoroughly creamed with an equal quantity of water or soymilk before using.

> *750 gm wholemeal wheat flour*
> *2 tablespoons tahina or sesame paste*
> *15 gm salt or 30 gm miso (soya bean paste)*
> *15 gm yeast*
> *2¹/₅-2¹/₄ cups water*

Rub the tahina or creamed sesame paste into the flour/salt mixture. If using miso dissolve it in a little of the water. Proceed as in Recipe 16. Roll the loaf in plenty of sesame seeds before tinning.

Creamed sunflower, peanut, hazelnut or cashew butters or pastes can be used instead of tahina or sesame paste in this recipe. The meals made from these nuts can also be used in bread for a delicious and unusual treat.

29 Sunflower bread

Lightly toast 2 cups of sunflower seeds in the oven until fragrant and golden. When cool, grind them to a coarse meal in an electric blender or coffee mill, or mortar and pestle. That wonderful mortar and pestle of the Japanese, the suribachi, is very efficient for this.

> *375 gm unbleached white flour*
> *375 gm 80 per cent wheat flour or 100 per cent*
>   *wholemeal*
> *15 gm salt*
> *1¹/₂ cups sunflower meal*
> *15 gm yeast*
> *2¹/₄ cups water (a little extra if wholemeal is used)*

Rub the sunflower meal into the flour and salt mixture and proceed as in Recipe 16. The loaf can be rolled in coarsely ground sunflower seeds before tinning.

30 Five grain bread

Wheat, rye, barley, rice and oats make this a substantial loaf with good flavour.

> *500 gm 80 per cent wheat flour or unbleached white flour*
> *250 gm sifted rye flour*
> *100 gm oat flour or fine oatmeal*
> *100 gm barley flour or fine meal*
> *15 gm salt*
> *15 gm yeast*
> *1 teaspoon liquid malt extract or pure malt powder*
> *150 gm cooked brown rice*
> *2-2²/₃ cups water*

Dissolve the malt with the yeast. Knead the rice in the water until milky. The method is the same as in Recipe 16. Roll the loaf or loaves in wheatmeal before tinning.

31 Soya bread — and really liked it!

This is not an unpleasantly gluggy health loaf as anything called soya often seems to be. It merely employs soya bean milk as a texture improver, flavour enhancer and alternative to cow's milk, which I do not use. Good soymilk is available commercially. It is relatively easy to make at home, but the process is too complex to describe here. Refer to *Natural Tucker,* chapter 12.

> *750 gm unbleached white flour, 80 per cent wheat flour or*
> *   100 per cent wholemeal wheat flour*
> *15 gm salt*
> *15 gm yeast*
> *150 gm cooked brown rice*
> *1 cup water*
> *1 cup soymilk (extra will be needed if using wholemeal*
> *   flour)*

Knead the rice with the water until milky, mix in the soymilk. Proceed as in Recipe 16.

Whole soymilk without any water can be used for making rolls. You will need a tablespoon or two more for the dough, than if you use plain water, see page 65.

32 Soya wheat bread (ii)

Somewhat unorthodox but good eating, this bread uses soya bean curd or tofu, see page 37, to achieve the same result (almost) as is obtained by using cream. Some bakers add cream to wholemeal bread because it improves the texture of the dough and adds richness to the flavour. Puree the tofu in a blender or thoroughly mash it first.

> *750 gm wholemeal wheat flour*
> *15 gm salt*
> *15 gm yeast*
> *4 tablespoons pureed tofu*
> *$2^1/5$ cups water*

Mix the tofu in with the water and follow the directions for Recipe 16. Roll the dough in sesame seeds before tinning.

33   Soya wheat bread (iii)

A soft (for stoneground wholemeal) and flavoursome soya bread can be made from the following ingredients:

500 gm wholemeal wheat flour
15 gm salt
15 gm yeast
150 gm pureed tofu
1 cup warm water

Directions are the same as Recipe 32.

34   Leaven flavoured, yeast boosted wheat bread

This bread is well worth the effort and always receives favourable comment. The yeast and leaven doughs are best made separately as this gives the leaven an opportunity to become active and produce its characteristic flavour. It is a simple matter to knead the two doughs together when they reach maturity.

(a)   *500 gm wholemeal wheat flour*
       1/2 teaspoon salt
       1 1/2 cups leaven
       1/2 cup water

(b)   *500 gm unbleached white flour*
       10 gm salt
       10 gm yeast
       1 1/3 cups water

Make up dough (a) according to Recipe 1 and dough (b) to Recipe 20. This recipe uses olive oil and malt extract but the method is the same. Leave both of the doughs for 3 hours to prove, then thoroughly knead the two until fully amalgamated. Divide the dough and place in oiled tins to rise for 1 hour or until doubled in bulk. Bake at 205°C (400°F) for 45 minutes. Remove from the tin and bake a further 5 minutes.

Sifted rye flour can be substituted in dough (a). The result is a fine flavoured bread with a sour bite and the lightness of white flour. It is a good idea to use 750 gm unbleached white flour, 15 gm salt, 15 gm yeast and 1 3/4 cups water to make up the wheat dough. Use only half the rye dough, otherwise the rye is too dominant. The remaining rye dough can be refrigerated for further use, or dropped back into the mother leaven.

35   Scotch-bake bread

By far the best yeasted bread results from a dough which has matured for at least 12 hours using the minimum yeast. Scottish bakers have or had a marvellous method of producing exceptional bread with this technique. To justify what I call Scotch-bake you need a big family or lots of friends, because it cannot be made in batches of less than 4¹/₂ kilos of dough. It is most enjoyable to make and even more enjoyable to experience the reactions when it is tasted. See page 29 for information on the optimum temperatures for this process.

To begin:

(a)   *500 gm unbleached white flour*
       250 gm wholemeal wheat flour
       5 gm salt
       5 gm yeast
       2¹/₂ cups water

Mix the flours and salt in a large bowl. Cream the yeast in a little of the water. Add this to the flour with the rest of the water and mix well. This is a soft or sticky dough. Flour hands and knead briefly for a good mix. Allow to stand, covered, for 12 hours. It should be very active by then.

Then:

(b)   *500 gm unbleached white flour*
       500 gm wholemeal flour
       15 gm salt
       2 teaspoons liquid malt extract
       *   or pure malt powder*
       5 cups water

Mix the flours and salt. Dissolve the malt extract or pure powder in a little water. Add to dough (a) with 5 cups water. This makes a mass which is difficult to manage. Stir vigorously with a wooden spoon and, when your strength gives out, plunge oiled hands into the bowl and mix until elastic gluten strands are evident. It is easier to remove dough from oiled hands! Cover and allow to rise for 2 to 3 hours until strongly active.

Finally:

(c)   *1 kilo 80 per cent wheat flour*
       25 gm salt
       3 tablespoons olive oil
       ³/4 cup water

Mix the wheat flour and salt and add to dough (b) with 3 tablespoons olive oil and ³/4 cup water. It requires thorough kneading to form a smooth dough. Add more water or flour if necessary. Cover and allow to rise 1 hour. Divide into six or seven loaves. Place in oiled tins, half filling each tin. When the dough reaches the top of the tin, or at least doubles in bulk, bake at 220°C (425°F) for 40 to 45 minutes.

If your oven doesn't house so many loaves, divide off half the dough before the final rising. Cover it or place it in a plastic bag and refrigerate. When the risen half goes into the oven, tin the refrigerated half and it should be risen by the time the first three have come out. Yes, it's a lengthy and adventurous procedure. Obviously it must be worth it!

Scotch-bake bread can be made with a number of different flour combinations, but keep the wholemeal proportion at or under half of the total weight of the flour. The same applies to 80 per cent flour, unless you have sifted it yourself from bread flour made from hard wheat. This bread is also very good made entirely from unbleached white flour or by adding 80 per cent flour in the (c) stage and using unbleached white for the rest.

36   Granary bread

If you like the malt flavour, this loaf is for you. It employs malted bran which is not widely available, but can be found in some health food stores. Malted bran is marketed by Roberts Soy products.

> *350 gm unbleached white flour*
> *250 gm 80 per cent flour*
> *100 gm malted bran*
> *15 gm yeast*
> *15 gm salt*
> *1¹/₂ cups warm water*
> *2 tablespoons unrefined oil*
> *100 gm cooked brown rice or barley*

Blend the flours and bran well. Cream the yeast in a little of the water. Dissolve the salt in the remaining water and whisk with the oil. Add the yeast liquid to the flour along with the water, salt, oil and rice. Mix well with a wooden spoon and bring the dough together with your hands. Re-knead for 1 minute and place in an oiled tin, half full. This will reach the top of the tin in 45 minutes to 1 hour. Bake at 220°C (425°F) for 40 minutes.

37   Herb bread

This is good with cheese and wine! The herbs must be subtle, not overpowering as some herb breads tend to be.

> *500 gm unbleached white flour*
> *250 gm 80 per cent flour*
> *100 gm wholemeal rye flour*
> *1 teaspoon whole aniseeds*
> *1 tablespoon crushed coriander seeds*
> *1 tablespoon chopped fresh rosemary*
> *20 gm yeast*
> *20 gm salt*
> *A little over 1³/₄ cups water*

Blend the flours well with the seeds and herb. Cream the yeast with a little of the water. Dissolve the salt in the remaining water. Add the yeast liquid and water with the salt to the flours and mix well with a wooden spoon. Knead the dough for 2 to 3 minutes. Cover and allow to rise for 1 hour. Reshape the loaf into a high oval. Cover and let rise 45 minutes to 1 hour. Gently prick the loaf seven times through its depth with a skewer. Bake at 220°C (425°F) for 35 to 40 minutes.

UNLEAVENED BREADS

Generally, cut the surface of an unleavened loaf to a depth of 1 cm, perhaps in a decorative pattern. This allows the loaf to expand without cracking.

38 Whole grain bread
This is an easy way to make a good tasting loaf.

(a)   *2 cups wholemeal wheat flour*
       2¹/₂ cups 80 per cent wheat' flour
       2 teaspoons salt
       4 cups cooked whole grain (buckwheat, rice, millet, barley)
       2 cups water

or
(b)   *2 cups 80 per cent wheat flour*
       1¹/₂ cups corn or maize meal
       1 cup buckwheat or barley flour
       2 teaspoons salt
       4 cups cooked whole grain
       2 cups water

Mix the flours and salt. Add the grain to the water and break up any lumps. Mix water and grain with the flour and beat with a spoon. This should be more of a batter than a dough. Put in an oiled tin so that the batter almost reaches the top. Bake at 180°C (350°F) for 50 minutes.

39 Bread of ages

This bread is not strictly an unleavened bread, because it does rise. However, the rise is spontaneously generated from within, so perhaps it should be entitled self-leavened bread. When I first made this bread, my son, who usually shows a preference for yeasted breads, developed a passion for it as though he had never eaten before! He thought it was the best he had ever tasted and could we have it all the time, please? The recipe is in a pamphlet entitled *Bread's Biological Trans-mutations* by Louis C. Kervran, a well known bio-scientist, and Jacques de Langre.* I have modified it to produce two loaves about 650 gm each.

> *1 kilo wholemeal wheat flour (Kervran specifies that the flour should have been ground no longer than 24 hours before use and should be from sound organic or biodynamic wheat.)*
> *1¹/₂ tablespoons unrefined oil (corn, sesame, olive)*
> *2 teaspoons salt*
> *3 cups warm water*

Rub the oil into the flour. Dissolve the salt in a little of the water. Add the salted water and the remaining water to the flour. Knead the dough to 'the consistency of putty or a fleshy earlobe . . . Knead in a spirallic motion, avoid up and down pumping'. Add more water if necessary. Place the dough in an earthenware, wooden or crockery bowl, cover and leave for 12 to 36 hours to prove. Twenty-four hours is usually sufficient. If the dough appears to be rising after 8 hours, especially in summer, knead briefly 'to release the by-product of gases . . . which would sour the dough if left in'.

Divide the dough and form into loaves. Place in oiled tins. Preheat the oven to 50°C (120°F) and put a large bowl of boiling water in the bottom. Leave the loaves in the oven for 45 minutes. Remove them to a warm spot and cover. Heat the oven to 190°C (375°F). Slash the loaves their full length and through half their depth. Take out the pan of water and bake the bread for ¹/₂ hour. Lower the oven to 180°C (350°F) and bake a further 20 minutes until a 'cherry-wood colour' crust forms. 'Do not underbake as unbaked starches are indigestible.' There should be a 'sharp, solid sound' when the loaf is tapped on the bottom.

* Published by Happiness Press, California.

40　Tibetan barley bread

I have yet to establish the authenticity of this bread. Poorer Tibetans probably just use barley flour and water. At any rate it is delicious, and those of you who have a taste for the authentic and enjoy chewing will relish it.

400 gm barley flour
400 gm wholemeal wheat flour
1 teaspoon salt
2 tablespoons unrefined oil (light sesame is the best)
2²/3 cups boiling water

Lightly toast 200 gm of the barley flour in the oven until just coloured and sweet smelling. Mix with the rest of the barley flour, wheat flour and salt. Rub in the oil. Add the boiling water and mix with a wooden spoon until a dough forms. Knead the hot dough until smooth. Hands can be kept cool by plunging them in a bowl of cold water. Form into one large or two small loaves, in oiled tins or free standing. Cover and leave overnight to prove. Slash the length of the loaf through half of its depth, or turn the round shape from its bowl and prick with a skewer ten times. Bake at 205°C (400°F) for 1 hour. Untin and bake a further 10 minutes. The round loaf can be removed after 1 hour. The crust is unique and crisscrossed with hairline cracks.

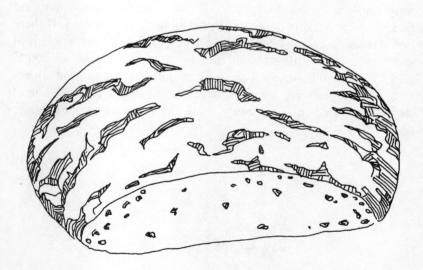

41 Essene bread

According to the Essene gospel of St John, wheat sprout bread, unleavened and baked in the sun, was consumed by that ancient sect of mystics.

'Moisten your wheat that the angel of water may enter it . . . and the blessing . . . will soon make the germ of life to sprout . . . then crush your grain and make thin wafers as did your forefathers . . .

These people are significant in that it is thought Jesus spent much time with them. They practised a pure diet and ritual bathing (as did John the Baptist). If you have the time and the skill to bake this bread in the sun as they did, enjoy it. For this, you must spread the dough paper thin in very hot sunlight.

This recipe is destined for a modern oven. Essene bread is available all over the USA, being made on the west coast of Canada at Richmond. It is sweet, sticky and very enjoyable, although different from any other bread. Crushing the wheat sprouts is quite an operation and I have still to find a suitable method. I suspect the Samap hand-mill would be a very useful tool for this purpose. A Corona metal-burr hand-mill works well, although I think the sprouts should be stonemilled. Failing these two tools, I have ground the sprouts a little at a time in an electric blender. This is only satisfactory. If you are using this method, make sure the sprouts are not too finely blended. They should be crushed not liquidised.

Use 1 kilo five day old wheat sprouts (see page 44). Crush the sprouts until each individual grain is broken, and form into two round loaves. Make the shape domed as this dough tends to spread. If there is liquid running everywhere from the crushing, add a little wholemeal wheat flour. Ideally this should not be necessary. Bake at 100°C (212°F) for 5 to 6 hours until the crust is quite brown and the underside of the loaf is very brown. Leave for 12 hours to cure. Cut it with a wet serrated knife or simply break and share with your friends.

42 Gluten-free bread

100 per cent rye and barley breads are suitable for those on a gluten-free diet. Though both of these contain gluten, it is not wheat gluten.

A tasty bread can also be made from a mixture of flours and requires minimal kneading.

(a)   *250 gm rye flour*
        100 gm millet meal
        100 gm barley flour
        100 gm oat flour
        2 tablespoons miso
        1 cup rye or barley leaven
        1 cup cooked brown rice
        1 cup water
or
(b)   *250 gm rye flour*
        100 gm millet meal
        100 gm barley flour
        100 gm oat flour
        2 teaspoons sea salt
        15 gm yeast
        1 cup cooked brown rice
        1³/4 cups water

Thoroughly mix the flours with sea salt or dissolve the miso in a little of the water and add with the remaining water. Add the leaven or yeast, rice and water. Bring the dough together with your hands and mix well. Form into a loaf shape with floured hands and place in an oiled tin. Dough (a) should two-thirds fill the tin. Cover and prove for 4 to 6 hours to reach the top of the tin. Bake at 205°C (400°F) for 55 minutes. Remove from the tin and bake a further 5 minutes.

The yeasted variety, dough (b), should two-thirds fill the tin and will rise to the top of the tin in 1 hour. Baking directions are the same.

or
(c) The same ingredients can be used for an unleavened loaf. Omit leaven or yeast and use 2 cups water. Miso tastes better than salt in this loaf. Cut decorative slashes on the surface. Bake at 205°C (400°F) for 1 hour.

SPECIAL BREADS

43 Spicy fruit bread

As with all the special breads, the type of flour used can be varied. As long as you remember that the amount of liquid needed will alter depending on the flour, 80 per cent can be used entirely or in combination with wholemeal or unbleached white flours.

500 gm wholemeal wheat flour
500 gm 80 per cent wheat flour
2 teaspoons salt
1 tablespoon cinnamon
1 teaspoon allspice
1/2 teaspoon nutmeg
25 gm yeast
1 tablespoon honey or maple syrup
1 teaspoon finely grated ginger root
1 teaspoon liquid malt extract
Juice of 1 lemon
Finely grated rind of 1 lemon
3 tablespoons unrefined oil
2 1/2 cups apple juice and water in equal quantities
1 cup sultanas
1 cup currants

Liquify the yeast with a little of the apple juice, the honey and ginger. Dissolve the malt in lemon juice and add the rind. Mix together thoroughly the flour(s), salt and spices. Add the yeast mixture to the flour and mix in with a wooden spoon. Whisk the oil with the lemon juice-malt-rind mix and stir. Add the apple juice-water to make a slightly sticky dough. Mix in sultanas and currants. You may have trouble incorporating the dried fruit in the dough. There are two options: either soak the fruit for 15 minutes in warm water before using or dredge well with flour. Knead for 5 minutes to form a soft dough which is still a little sticky.

Cover and allow 1 hour to rise. Re-knead and place in oiled tins. Cover for the final rise of 45 minutes or leave until double in size. Bake at 220°C (425°F) for 45 minutes.

Of course, this recipe can easily be made with leaven. Use 2 cups of leaven instead of yeast, 1 teaspoon of salt and $1^1/_2$ cups of apple juice-water. The other ingredients remain the same. Two-thirds fill the oiled tins with dough, cover, allow to fill the tin (the proving will take 4 to 6 hours) and bake at 205°C (400°F) for 1 hour.

This recipe can also be used to make buns. Roll out the dough 2.5 cm (1 inch) thick with a rolling pin. Cut out your choice of shapes with a dough cutter or drinking glass. Glaze, (see Recipe 36), allow to rise and bake at 220°C (425°F) for 12 to 15 minutes.

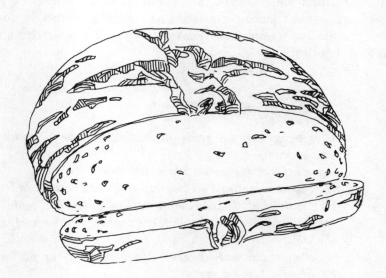

44 Barm-brack

'Brack', which is spelt in various ways, is a Celtic word used to describe the interplay of light on a gemstone something like our word 'sparkling'. In Barm-brack it refers to the glistening of the currants when the bread is sliced.

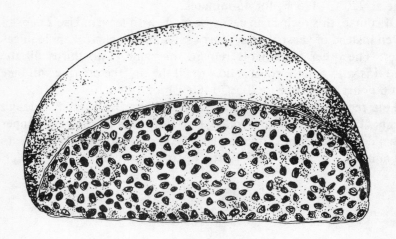

Barm is a beer yeast, but you can substitute any wheat leaven if you don't have or can't make barm (see page 45). Barm-brack is traditionally made as a round so use a cake tin or rise it in a wooden bowl and turn it out for baking.

550 gm 80 per cent wheat flour
1 teaspoon salt
2-4 teaspoons caraway seeds, depending on your tolerance
2 cups currants
1 cup ale-barm leaven or wheat leaven
2 tablespoons unrefined oil (Unsalted ripened butter can be used instead of oil and is more authentic. Use 3-5 tablespoons and reduce the water quantity in the recipe slightly.)
2 tablespoons unrefined honey or pure maple syrup plus a little more for glazing
1 tablespoon liquid malt extract
Finely grated rind and juice of 1 lemon
1 cup water

The texture of this dough is between a cake and bread. It must be sticky, so mix with a wooden spoon. Mix flour, salt, seeds and currants. Dissolve the sweeteners in a little of the water with lemon juice and rind. Add barm, oil and sweeteners with water to the flour. Mix well. Add the remaining water and mix until smooth. (Omit the oil and add the butter before the final addition of water if you are using butter.)

The dough should two-thirds fill an oiled cake tin or floured wooden bowl. Cover and allow 3 to 5 hours to rise. If your leaven is at a particularly active and sweet stage, the quantity employed here can be doubled and the water quantity reduced by $1/3$ cup. This will give a good rise and pleasant flavour if the dough does not have to mature too long. Bake at 205°C (400°F) for 40 to 50 minutes. Glaze when hot with honey or maple syrup.

45 Brioche

Cath, a dear friend who is half of the Feedwell Café, asked if this recipe was to be included as she had fond memories of it. As with croissants, I think it is a more wholesome version than those sugary things loaded with all sorts of dubious and unnecessary additives which can be bought from most bakers. More to the point, perhaps, it tastes excellent and will be an indication to you how far some bakers stray from the authentic ingredients. The use of soymilk is hardly traditional, however, so use cow's milk, if you like. Soymilk is a worthy substitute because it has a similar effect on dough as cow's milk, but does not have the saturated fat and cholesterol of cow's milk.

280 gm unbleached white flour or 80 per cent wheat flour
1 teaspoon salt
10 gm yeast
1 teaspoon honey or pure maple syrup
2 tablespoons soymilk
3 eggs at room temperature
1 tablespoon finely grated lemon rind
Juice of ¹/₂ lemon
150 gm unsalted ripened butter at room temperature
Egg yolk, maple syrup or honey for glazing

Thoroughly blend the salt and flour. Dissolve the yeast in the soymilk with the honey and add to the flour mixture with the lemon rind and lemon juice. Whisk the eggs briefly and beat into the mixture. Rub in the butter with your hands until a very soft dough is formed. Cover and allow to rise for 2 hours until very active. Stir the dough with a wooden spoon until deflated, place in a bowl, cover and leave in a cool spot 3 hours or overnight. The dough will double in size and again be very active. Overnight proving is best.

Mix well with a wooden spoon and place the dough in a well oiled tin. It should be half full. The traditional shape is round and brioche tins are available from kitchen supply shops, but I have risen brioche in all sorts of round containers from earthenware baking bowls to oval bread tins. The dough will take another 3 hours to rise — it should nearly reach the top of the tin so be sure to use an appropriate sized container. Make a deep, circular slash two centimetres or so in from the edge of the tin.

Allow a minute to recover from cutting and bake at 190°C (375°F) for 20 to 25 minutes. Glaze with an egg yolk or maple syrup or honey.

Egg yolk gives the darkest crust, but maple syrup gives an excellent sheen. Return to the oven for 5 minutes. The mushroomed top will now be shining, well risen and very appetising.

I am indebted to Simone Beck and Julia Child's *Mastering the Art of French Cooking* (Penguin, Middlesex, England) and Elizabeth David's *English Bread and Yeast Cookery* (Penguin) for the inspiration to bake an authentic (well nearly) brioche. Even though some of the ingredients I use are totally heretical, they are at least innocent.

46 Croissants

Baking croissants is a somewhat formidable undertaking. I include them here because I am a devotee who has tired of the pap presented by many a baker or patisserie. Croissants *have* to be made with unsalted ripened butter and *have* to be given a dough maturation period of at least 8 hours. The insidious ingredients that go into some croissants have to be seen or tasted to be believed. It is the same dreary tale as bread.

This recipe is adapted from Simone Beck and Julia Child's *Mastering the Art of French Cooking*. I have replaced refined cane sugar with a mixture of pure honey and liquid malt extract, cow's milk with soymilk and the flour with unbleached white or a mixture of one-third 80 per cent flour and two-thirds unbleached white. As in the Brioche recipe, my substitutions are unorthodox and probably horrifying to some. The results are very good, however, and the replacement of sugar with honey and malt makes the bread more wholesome. Croissants *can* be made with a proportion of wholemeal flour, see Recipe 49, although the classic flaky texture and crispness are to some extent lost.

This recipe will yield two dozen croissants, making it possible to freeze some for other breakfasts. Thaw them in a moderate oven.

> *1 kilo unbleached white flour*
> *3¹/4 teaspoons salt*
> *15 gm yeast*
> *1 teaspoon liquid malt extract*
> *1 teaspoon pure honey*
> *280 ml (¹/2 pint) soymilk*
> *3 tablespoons mild tasting unrefined oil (do not use heavy, strongly flavoured oil)*
> *1 cup water*
> *Egg and water for glazing*
> *500 gm cold unsalted ripened butter*

In a small bowl, dissolve the yeast, malt and honey in a little of the water. Mix the salt and flour. Add the yeast-malt-honey mixture, soymilk and oil to the flour along with the water and mix thoroughly with a wooden spoon. This is a sticky dough. Leave to stand covered, for 10 minutes.

Gently knead so as not to overdevelop the gluten, but to mix the ingredients completely. Set aside in a bowl enclosed in a large plastic bag, sealed, for 3 hours. The dough will triple in bulk. Gently re-knead on a lightly floured board. Form into a rectangle 46 cm x 30 cm (18 x 12 inches). Fold into three with the two 15 cm (6 inch) pieces at either end overlapping the middle third one. Cover and let rise 1¹/₂ hours. After this proving, turn the dough out onto a lightly floured tray, enclose in a plastic bag and refrigerate for 40 minutes. Careful refrigeration is necessary at all stages of production during hot weather.

Take the butter out of the refrigerator or cellar. It must be cold. With a rolling pin, spatula and heel of hand pressure, work the butter until smooth. It must stay cold. Re-refrigerate if it goes soft or oily.

Flour your hands and gently flatten the dough into a rectangle. Roll out lightly with a rolling pin to form a 46 cm x 30 cm (12 x 18 inch) rectangle with the 30 cm border closest and furthest from you. Spread the butter over the upper two-thirds of the rectangle. Do not butter 6 mm (¹/₄ inch) around the border so you can seal the butter inside an envelope when it is folded. Fold the lower, unbuttered third of the dough into one-third of the buttered layer. Fold the remaining one-third of buttered dough over this. Flour the board and dough and carefully roll out to its original 46 x 30 cm size. Fold the dough in thirds again, starting with the 30 cm border furthest from you. Cover and refrigerate 3 hours.

Turn out the cold dough onto a lightly floured surface. Roll out into the 46 cm x 30 cm size. Fold the dough into thirds, cover and refrigerate 3 hours or overnight. If left overnight at this stage, you can rise early to make and bake the croissants for a heartwarming breakfast.

Roll the dough out 25 cm x 50 cm (10 x 20 inches) and cut into four 12 x 25 cm (5 x 10 inch) pieces. Refrigerate the pieces not being used. Roll out each piece to 12 cm x 39 cm (5 x 15 inches). Divide into three 12 x 12 cm (5 x 5 inch) squares and cut each of these from corner to corner, making six triangles.

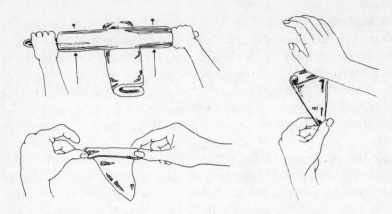

Form each triangle into a croissant. To do this you must have an idea of what a croissant looks like. I watched a patissier do this most mornings for twelve months while I hid behind my coffee in the front of his shop. Start with the apex of the triangle pointing towards you. Hold the apex with your left hand and, with your right hand, roll the base of the triangle over one tight turn. While holding the rolled base with the heel of your right hand, gently pull the apex of the triangle towards you. This elongates the triangle. At the same time as you pull gently, roll up the triangle with the heel of your right hand.

Curl the points of the shape into a characteristic crescent. Set on an oiled baking sheet, cover and leave to rise until double in bulk. This should take no more than 1 hour. Brush with a glaze made from equal quantities of egg and water. Bake at 230°C (450°F) for 12 to 15 minutes.

The croissants can be frozen for a few days when set on the tray before the final rise. Thaw in a low oven before baking.

47 Croissant on a leaven

Knowing that croissants were made before the introduction of modern yeast, I thought it should be possible to use an appropriate leaven instead. The results were very successful with a good rise and excellent flavour. The preparation time needs to be shortened because leaven tends to make the dough slack (more liquid) if left for as long a proving as yeasted croissant dough.

> *1 kilo unbleached white flour*
> *2 teaspoons salt*
> *1¹/2 cups wholemeal leaven*
> *1 teaspoon liquid malt extract*
> *1 teaspoon pure honey*
> *280 ml (¹/2 pint) soymilk*
> *3 tablespoons unrefined oil (this must not be strongly flavoured)*
> *¹/3 cup water*

The basic steps are the same as in Recipe 46, but the timing is quite different. After making the first rectangle, fold and refrigerate 1 hour. Add the butter as in Recipe 46 and refrigerate 2 hours. Roll out and fold twice. Refrigerate 3 hours or overnight. Roll out, cut, shape, rise. Bake 5 minutes longer than Recipe 46 in a 220°C (425°F) oven.

48 Raisin croissant

Proceed as in Recipe 46. When shaping the croissant, place about 8 raisins or seeded muscatels on the base of the shape and roll them in the dough as you form the shape.

49 Wholemeal croissant

As mentioned in Recipe 46, croissants can be made with a proportion of wholemeal flour. This should not exceed fifty per cent of the total flour. It can be blended with unbleached white or eighty per cent cake flour; of course, a little extra water is required for the dough if wholemeal is used. The results are delicious — not as light as the standard recipe, with less characteristic layering, but what is lost in cosmetic appeal is more than made up in flavour. The Feedwell Café, 95 Greville Street, Prahran, Melbourne, serves this and other delights on Saturday mornings.

50   Fruit and nut bread

550 gm 80 per cent wheat flour
1 cup almond meal or 1¹/2 cups chopped toasted almonds
15 gm yeast
2 tablespoons pure maple syrup
2 tablespoons oil
2 teaspoons finely grated orange rind
Juice of 1 orange
1 teaspoon salt
2 cups sultanas (if you are using natural sultanas, sun-dried
  and chemical free, soak for ¹/2 hour before using them.)
1 cup warm water

Dissolve the yeast in a little of the water with the maple syrup. Mix the orange rind with the juice and salt. Thoroughly blend the almonds and flour. Add the yeast mixture to the flour and mix well, followed by the oil, orange mixture and sultanas. Stir in the remaining water with a wooden spoon until a soft dough forms. With floured hands, knead the dough for a few minutes until smooth. It should be a soft or slightly sticky dough. Place in a bowl, cover and allow 1 hour to rise in a warm spot. This dough will increase in volume by one-third. The dough is difficult to manage, so reshape it and put it into an oiled tin. Cover and bake when the dough increases in bulk by one-third, in a 205°C (400°F) oven for 55 minutes.

51   Apricot and buckwheat bread

400 gm 80 per cent wheat flour
150 gm buckwheat flour
³/4 teaspoon nutmeg
1 teaspoon salt
15 gm yeast
1 teaspoon liquid malt extract
2 tablespoons unrefined oil
1 cup warm apple juice
1 teaspoon pure vanilla extract
¹/2 cup warm water
1 cup chopped dried apricots soaked for ¹/2 hour in water

Mix the flours thoroughly with nutmeg and salt. Dissolve the yeast in a little of the water with the malt. Whisk or blend together the oil, apple juice, vanilla and remaining water. Add yeast to the flours and mix well. Stir in the apple juice mixture and the apricots. Mix well with a wooden spoon and then hand mix it. This is a sticky dough. Cover and allow 1 hour to rise in a warm place. Re-shape and tin. This dough will increase in volume by one-third. Bake at 205°C (400°F) for 45 minutes or 1 hour if necessary.

52   Apple and walnut bread

> *500 gm wholemeal wheat flour*
> *1 cup leaven or barm*
> *2 tablespoons unrefined oil*
> *1 teaspoon salt*
> *¹/2 cup warm water*
> *1 tablespoon pure honey*
> *¹/2 cup apple juice*
> *1 cup coarsely chopped walnuts*
> *2 medium sized apples coarsely grated*
> *3 teaspoons cinnamon*
> *Pinch cloves*
> *200 gm raisins*

Dissolve the salt in the water. Stir the barm into the flour. Mix the oil, salt and water, honey and apple juice (whisk together or emulsify in a blender). Add to the flour with the walnut, apples, spices and raisins. Using a wooden spoon, bring the mixture together to form a soft or slightly sticky dough. Two-thirds fill an oiled tin and cover. In a suitable warm spot, this should rise sufficiently in 3 to 4 hours. Bake at 205°C (400°F) for 45 minutes.

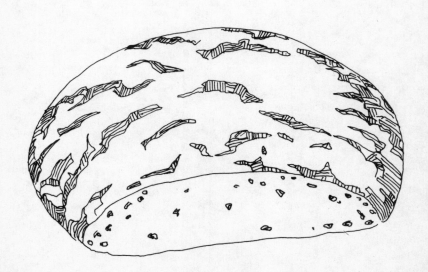

53   Maple-walnut bread

500 gm wholemeal wheat flour
1 cup leaven or barm
1 teaspoon salt
¹/₂ cup water
3 tablespoons unrefined oil
¹/₂ cup pure maple syrup plus a little more for glazing
1 cup coarsely chopped walnuts
1 tablespoon pure vanilla extract

Dissolve the salt in the water. Whisk together with oil or blend. Mix barm or leaven into the flour until evenly dispersed. Add the salt-water-oil mixture to the flour along with the maple syrup, walnuts and vanilla. Either with your hands or with a wooden spoon, form into a soft, sticky dough. Two-thirds fill an oiled tin and cover. Set in a warm place to rise for 4 to 6 hours. The dough should reach the top of the tin. Bake at 205°C (400°F) for 45 minutes. Brush the top with maple syrup and return to the oven for 5 minutes.

54   Coconut bread

500 gm unbleached white flour
15 gm yeast
¹/₃ cup water
4 tablespoons palm sugar (see Glossary)
2 teaspoons salt
1 cup unsweetened coconut milk (canned or fresh)
  (see page 37)
1 cup fresh grated or dessicated coconut

Dissolve the yeast in the water with the palm sugar. Mix the salt and coconut milk. Add the yeast and water to the flour and distribute evenly with a wooden spoon, followed by the coconut milk and coconut. This will form a soft, smooth dough. Place in a bowl, cover and allow 1 hour to rise in a warm spot. The dough will increase in volume by two-thirds. Re-knead gently, mould, and tin the dough. Cover and allow to double in volume. Bake at 220°C (425°F) for 35 to 40 minutes.

55   The east is bread

Rudyard Kipling spoke too soon. East and west can meet in bread where tofu or soya bean curd beloved in the east are a more than adequate substitute for western dairy products in baking. Lecithin (another soy derivative) has long been known as bread improver, as is soya flour in certain combinations. Tofu provides the moisture and crumb characteristics of milk, cream or eggs. The advantage of tofu is that, while having a high protein rating (a good range of essential amino acids which are complemented by the protein of wheat), it does not contain any saturated fat or cholesterol. Apart from its use as a substitute, I think tofu can stand alone as a bread improver or an ingredient in cakes.

325 gm wholemeal wheat flour
1 teaspoon salt
$^1/_2$ teaspoon cinnamon
1 cup barm or leaven
300 gm (10$^1/_2$ oz) tofu (Prepackaged Morinaga silken tofu is just the right size. It is available from Asian groceries and some health food stores. Fresh tofu is of better quality.)
$^1/_4$ cup unrefined oil
$^1/_4$ cup maple syrup
Finely grated rind of 1 lemon
Juice of $^1/_2$ lemon
1 cup apple puree
1 cup coarsely chopped walnuts
200 gm raisins

In a vitamiser, blend the tofu, oil, maple syrup, lemon peel and lemon juice.

Mix the flour, salt and cinnamon. Add barm or leaven to the flour and stir in thoroughly. Add the tofu mixture and apple puree followed by walnuts and raisins. Blend well with a wooden spoon. Spoon into a shallow oiled tin, filling the tin two-thirds, cover and allow 3-4 hours to rise in a warm spot. Bake at 190ºC (375ºF) for 50 to 60 minutes. Is it cake or bread, Marie Antoinette?

56   Frumenty bread

100 gm fine (sifted) rye flour
500 gm wholemeal wheat flour
100 gm oat flour
1 teaspoon salt
2 cups leaven
1 cup grape juice
2 tablespoons unrefined oil
1 teaspoon orange or mandarin peel, grated or very finely
   chopped
¹/₂ cup water
200 gm cooked barley or other whole grain
2 cups raisins, sultanas and currants mixed

Mix the flours and salt thoroughly. Stir in the leaven until well distributed. Whisk or blend together the grape juice, oil, orange peel and water. Add to the flour and stir in. When a soft dough has formed, add the barley and dried fruit. Incorporate these into the dough. Mix with your hands and knead briefly. Place in an oiled tin, filling the tin two-thirds, cover and allow to rise for 3 to 4 hours. Bake at 205°C (400°F) for 50 minutes.

57   Wheat sprout and raisin unleavened bread

675 gm wholemeal wheat flour
1 teaspoon salt or 1 tablespoon white miso
2 teaspoons allspice
2 tablespoons oil
¹/₂ cup water
2 cups apple or grape juice
3 cups wheat sprouts
2 cups raisins

Carefully separate the wheat sprouts. Mix the salt and allspice with the flour. Whisk together or blend oil and water, and add to the flour with the juice. Incorporate wheat sprouts and raisins and stir with a wooden spoon until a sticky dough is formed. If using miso, add it with the oil and water. Place in an oiled tin, cover and allow to stand for 15 minutes before baking at 190°C (375°F) for 60 minutes.

58 Seventeenth century egg bread

This recipe is quoted in Elizabeth David's *English Bread and Yeast Cookery* (Penguin). It was so fascinating that I had to try it. The results were marvellous and particularly thrilled my father who claims not to be able to eat commercial bread any more!

> *500 gm unbleached white flour or 80 per cent wheat flour*
> *15 gm salt*
> *15 gm yeast*
> *1¹/₂ cups water or water and soymilk mixed in equal quan-*
>   *tities*
> *The whites of 2 eggs*

Dissolve the yeast in a little water. Mix the flour and salt. Add the yeast-water to the flour and mix well. Lightly beat the egg whites until just frothy and stir into the flour. Add the rest of the water and bring the dough together with a wooden spoon. Knead until smooth (5 minutes for unbleached white flour and 2 to 3 minutes for 80 per cent flour). Place in a bowl, cover and allow 1 hour to rise in a warm spot. The dough will double in volume. Re-knead and place in floured bowl (see page 61) with the seam facing upwards. Cover with the oiled baking sheet on which the bread will be baked and allow 30 minutes to rise. The dough will double in volume again. Turn the dough out and slash decisively. Let the dough recover for 1 minute and bake in a 220°C (425°F) oven for 30 minutes. This bread is also excellent risen in a tin, but it must be given a final rising of about 45 minutes before baking.

59   Challah — Jewish egg bread

For those who observe Jewish dietary laws, this bread can be eaten with meat meals as it does not contain cow's milk. It is an attractive and delicious treat.

600 gm unbleached white flour or 80 per cent wheat flour
3 teaspoons salt
20 gm yeast
$1/2$ cup warm soymilk mixed with $1/4$ cup warm water
3 tablespoons honey or pure maple syrup
2 eggs at room temperature
3 tablespoons olive oil
Egg yolk for glazing

Dissolve the yeast in the water-soymilk mixture with the honey. Add salt to the flour and mix well. Beat the eggs and whisk into the yeast mixture. Stir this into the flour and, when well mixed, blend in the oil. Knead well to form a smooth dough. Place in a bowl, cover and set in a warm place to rise. Allow to double in volume; this should take $1\frac{1}{2}$ hours. Re-knead well until all the gas has been expelled.

Cut the dough into three pieces. Each piece should be rolled out to form a long cylinder about 38 cm (15 inches) long. These are braided or plaited to form the traditional shape. Plaiting can be started at one end or in the middle, but the best results come from beginning in the middle. When plaiting is completed, place on an oiled baking sheet, cover and let rise for 30 minutes. Make a glaze by mixing an egg yolk with twice its volume of water. Brush the loaf thoroughly and bake at 190°C (375°F) for 15 minutes. Brush again with the egg mixture and bake another 15 minutes. The loaf should have a moist yellow crumb and a rich dark crust.

60   Steam bread

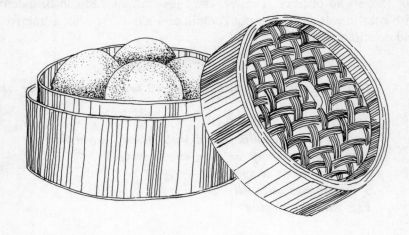

Loaves of bread can generally be steamed if no oven is available, but it is more efficient to make the dough into rolls or buns. This ancient cooking technique originated in northern China, where the buns are served plain or can be filled with a strong savoury or sweet mixture.

Unbleached white flour, 80 per cent cake flour or sifted wholemeal produce the best results.

(a)   With leaven
Consult Recipes 2, 3 or 4 for quantities. When dough is made, allow 2 hours to prove. Break up the dough into 100 gm pieces. Roll each into a ball and place on a small square of greaseproof paper. Set the balls in a Chinese bamboo steamer, allowing 2 cm clear space around each ball. Cover and allow 2 hours to prove. Bring water to a rapid boil in a saucepan or wok, put the lid on the steamer and place it over the water, which should be rapidly boiling for the whole process. The buns will be ready in 40 minutes.

(b)   With yeast
Consult Recipes 18 or 20 for quantities. Allow the dough to prove for 1 hour. Re-knead briefly and form into 100 gm balls. Proceed as for (a), but the buns will require 30 minutes to prove the second time. Steam as for (a), but for 30 minutes.

Fillings
When each ball is formed before the second proving, poke a hole in it and insert one tablespoon of filling, either savoury or sweet. Seal the

dough around the hole so the filling is completely enclosed, then set the balls in the steamer for final proving.

(a) Savoury
Chop 1 packet of tempeh (see Glossary) into small cubes. Fry in 3 tablespoons unrefined oil with 2 finely chopped cloves of garlic and 1 teaspoon of finely grated ginger root. When the tempeh is lightly browned, add 4 tablespoons of natural soy sauce (shoyu) and freshly ground black pepper. Mix and remove from the heat. This can be mashed slightly so it is easy to add to the buns.

(b) Sweet
Cook mung beans, red (azuki) beans, or any other common culinary bean, for example lima, until soft. (see *Natural Tucker,* pages 47-9). Strain so the beans are dry and mix in 2 tablespoons of palm sugar and 1 tablespoon dessicated coconut to each cup of beans.

There are many other savoury or sweet fillings for steam buns; a good Chinese cookbook will be a source of inspiration. See also *Natural Tucker,* pages 168-9.

GLOSSARY

Absorption Rate refers to the varying capacities of different flours to absorb water. For example, wholemeal flour absorbs more than white flour and wholemeals vary between themselves.

Atta Flour Lightly sifted wholemeal flour. It is usually 90-95 per cent extraction, which means 5-10 per cent of the whole flour has been removed as the coarsest bran.

Bashing is the act of deftly poking a hole in the top of a cottage loaf with a thumb — some bashers use their elbow!

Biodynamic A system of agriculture which promotes harmony between cultivated crops and the environment. This is done by the careful selection of companion plants and the use of herbal and mineral compounds for sprays and composting. Demeter products are usually B.D.

Biscuit Flour Flour which is more suited to biscuits and cakes than bread. See *cake flour*.

Bleached Flour After the bran and germ have been removed from milled wheat, the creamy coloured starch is usually treated with a range of chemical agents to mature, sterilise and whiten the flour. This process renders a flour more suitable for high speed machine handling and quick bread production. It is able to be used in mechanised processes as soon as it is bagged. Freshly ground, unbleached flour acquires stability through ageing at least 3 days and is unsuitable for a mechanised process if used immediately after it is ground. The bleaching of flour was therefore made necessary by the development of mechanised baking and mass storage of flour. Bleaching destroys most of the vitamins naturally contained in flour, most notably the B group.

Bread Flour is ground from hard, high protein wheat or medium-hard, medium protein wheat. It is more sandy in texture than flour ground from soft wheat. Bread flour is sometimes called strong flour. This flour enables a higher rise because it contains more gluten than soft wheat flour. See *gluten*.

Cake Flour is milled from soft, low protein wheat. Because it does not contain as much gluten as bread flour, this flour does not make an elastic dough. It cannot stretch or rise as much as a dough interlocked with a mass of gluten fibres. It is therefore not as suitable for bread as 'hard' flour — that is, flour milled from hard, high protein wheat. Lowan Wholefoods market a flour labelled Eighty per cent Cake Flour. See *Eighty per cent flour*.

Complete Protein Many foods abound in protein, but in order that the body can use it efficiently, eight different proteins, called amino acids, must be present. Meat and meat products contain all these amino acids, but the combination of cereal grain and legume also results in a complete protein.

Complex Carbohydrate is also called starch. Carbohydrate occurs naturally in simple or complex form. Simple carbohydrates are called sugars. Complex carbohydrate is made up of a large number of sugar molecules joined together. Complex carbohydrate is more slowly broken down during digestion and is a highly suitable food for man and leaven. Cereal grains are composed largely of complex carbohydrate.

Crust(y) The exterior surface of a baked loaf of bread. It varies from eggshell thin to thick and crunchy, depending on the type of flour, the humidity of the oven, the initial oven temperature and other factors. Crusty loaves are baked without an enclosing shape such as a tin to maximise the crust surface.

Crystal Malt Yellow granular powder which is a dried malt extract.

Eighty per cent (80 %) flour This means 20 per cent of the total 100 per cent (wholemeal) has been removed by sifting. The coarsest bran and some coarse germ constitute this 20 per cent. Most of the germ is intact, as are fine bran particles. See *extraction*.

Extraction refers to the percentage of flour which remains after 100 per cent wholemeal is sifted. The finest white flour is 65 per cent extraction which indicates 35 per cent of the bulk has been removed. Such flour would contain no bran or germ. Unbleached white flour is 70-75 per cent and the above-mentioned flour is 80 per cent. Home sifting produces about 80 per cent flour depending on the fineness of the sifter.

Fermentation The action of yeast digesting carbohydrate, respiring gases and producing an increase in dough temperature. The characteristic sign of fermentation beginning is the rising or aeration of dough.

Gluten The substance (protein) produced by the agitation of flour and water as in kneading. It is evident as elastic strands when a dough is stretched after kneading. Gluten gives dough elasticity and the ability to sustain a high rise. Soft flour is low in gluten and generally not used for bread today. Strong flour contains a higher percentage of gluten and produces well risen breads. Gluten flour, which is pure, powdered gluten, is often added to soft flour to make it more suitable for bread. See *bread flour*. See also page 20.

Hard Wheat Mainly grown in the northern USA, Canada and Ukraine, hard wheat contains a high proportion of protein and produces strong flour particularly suitable for mechanised bread production. Medium-hard wheats are produced in Australia. Hard wheat is usually dark, brown or red. Soft wheat is yellow or white.

Knead The action of rythmically manipulating a dough to produce good gluten formation and consequent elasticity. Brief kneading can be for the purpose of deflating a risen dough and expelling gases, so the yeast can be redistributed and continue its work. Kneading should be firm not violent. Doughs made from soft flour or cake flour require less kneading than strong flour dough as there is less gluten to form.

Leaven An agent used to aerate dough, which does not contain commercially prepared yeast or other rising agent. Leaven is a collection of yeasts which perform in a similar way to commercial yeast. It is usually spontaneously generated by the proliferation of wild yeasts from a mixture of flour and water and then renewed regularly with more flour and water to keep the yeasts alive. Leaven can be fed with certain foods, such as crushed wheat sprouts, which allow desirable yeasts to become dominant in the colony.

Liquid Malt Extract appears as a dark viscous liquid. Barley is sprouted, roasted and boiled in water. The water is then cooked or evaporated to produce this syrup. It is a valuable dough improver and yeast food if used in correct quantities.

Maturity refers to the age and degree of fermentation a dough has undergone. Flour is immature whereas a leaven can be called overmature. Mixing these two in the correct proportions results in a dough which is of adequate maturity for baking. See Recipe 5.

Meal Flour is distinguished from meal in that meal is more coarsely ground. The most suitable meal for use in breads is slightly more coarse than wholemeal flour. Meal suitable for breakfast porridge is too coarse for bread.

Miso is produced widely in Japan and eaten mainly as a soup stock.

Variations of it are made throughout Asia. Basically, miso results from fermenting soya beans, usually with a cereal grain such as barley. The ferment is aged with salt. Miso is a nutritious and flavoursome food.

Muffins Without getting into a controversy over terms, a muffin is a yeast risen, oil or fat enriched and slightly sweet cake. It is 2.5-3.5 cm (1-1¹/₂ inches) in diameter and 5 cm (2 inches) high. In Australia the muffin shape is the same as a 'scone' shape. Muffins are baked in an enclosing shape, which distinguishes them from scones.

Organic As there are no legal codes governing this label in Australia, organic is used to mean 'grown without the use of artificial chemical sprays, fertilisers, washes or dips'.

Palm Sugar A flavoursome natural sugar made from the sap which exudes from the buds of a special palm tree. This sap is boiled down to a dark, richly flavoured sugar. Usually sold in cylinders as Gula Java or 'coconut preserve', it is occasionally available in some Asian food stores.

Pastry Flour See *cake flour*.

Prove This refers to the period during which the dough is left to ferment and increase in volume.

Pure Malt Powder See *crystal malt*.

Roller Milling Instead of being ground between revolving circular stones, as in stone grinding, the wheat is usually ground between high speed rollers. These don't so much grind as tear the grain apart. The bran and germ are separated from the endosperm, which is then rolled to a fine powder, sifted and bleached.

Seam This term refers to a joint in the dough after moulding.

Slack This refers to dough texture. It is a soft dough which will flow or spread when left free standing. A stiff dough is more resilient and will maintain shape while free standing. Obviously, a soft dough contains more liquid component than a stiff dough. Dough becomes softer as it ferments.

Slash Cut the surface of a loaf as it is about to go in the oven. The cut is usually 3 cm (1 inch) deep.

Soft Flour See *bread flour*.

Soymilk This is an emulsion of soya beans and water made by soaking and grinding soya beans, cooking them with water, and straining off the grounds. The milky liquid which results is widely enjoyed in south-east and east Asia. When soymilk is curdled by the appropriate agent, it forms tofu or soya bean curd. Soymilk is nutritious and free from saturated fats or cholesterol. Ecologically, soymilk is far more efficient as a food source than cow's milk.

Stoneground Wheat is fed between two circular stones which revolve and crush the grain. Flour is spilled from the edge of the stones. Many claim that stoneground flour is superior in flavour to roller milled flour. Stone grinding is a more integral process than roller milling, preserving the essential nature of the wheat. All flour was stoneground until the nineteenth century.

Strong Flour See *bread flour*.

Tahina A paste made from ground, hulled sesame seeds. Sometimes oil is added, or emulsifying chemicals can be used. It is significant in Middle Eastern food, and in Asian cooking as a sesame puree. The Asian form is usually ground from toasted unhulled sesame seeds. It is often called Sesame Sauce in Asian groceries. When sesame puree is thoroughly mixed with a little water, a creamy paste results. This is suitable for use in bread. Tahina can be used in bread without mixing with water.

Tempeh A cultured soya bean product widely consumed in Indonesia. It is available from natural food stores and some Asian groceries. Tempeh is a very nutritious food, containing significant quantities of vitamin B12 and has a delicious almost meat-like flavour.

Tofu is the curd formed when soymilk is coagulated in much the same manner as cow's milk is separated into curds and whey. Tofu is widely eaten from Indonesia to Manchuria and from Burma to Japan. It is an ecologically efficient high protein food which does not contain saturated fats or cholesterol. Tofu cuisine is magnificent, as tofu is a bland medium of interesting and highly variable texture, which is an enhancing accompaniment to sauces and most other foods. This traditional food is now finding a home in the west and has interesting properties when used in breads.

Umeboshi Plum This is cultivated throughout east Asia. In Japan it is pickled in brine and Red Shiso (Beefsteak plant) leaves added. It is a marvellous natural medicine and is used in cooking.

Unbleached Flour As explained under bleached flour, most commercial flour is automatically sterilised and bleached as it comes from the roller mill. If this process is not carried out we have a creamy white flour which, depending on the sifting, contains a proportion of germ and some fine bran particles.

Alternatively, stoneground flour can be sifted through silk to form a creamy white unbleached flour. Unbleached flour is superior in flavour, colour and aroma to bleached white flour and is highly suitable for minimum mechanised or hand made bread.

Unrefined Oil Most cooking oil today is manufactured by various means of chemical or mechanical extraction. It is usually deodorised, bleached and adulterated with a preservative. Unrefined oil is pressed by traditional methods, and has not been treated chemically. It retains the essential flavour of the nut, seed, grain or fruit from which it was pressed and is nutritionally superior to commercial oils. It should be kept in a dark bottle and cool storage place. Some unrefined oils are too strong for use in bread.

Unsalted Butter is made from ripened (cultured) cream and is widely available. It is a better quality product than common commercial butter which is not ripened and contains a large proportion of salt. The culturing process gives ripened butter a rich flavour and higher food value as nutritive substances such as B vitamins are a by-product of culturing.

Wheatmeal can be coarsely ground wheat or, more usually, a wholemeal flour which has been roller milled. This means the bran and germ are separated from the starch during milling, and are remixed at a later stage. Labelling is indiscriminate in Australia and fortunately the term wheatmeal is not used widely, but many supposed wholemeals are really wheatmeals. Wheatmeals behave differently to genuine stoneground wholemeals.

Wholemeal Flour contains all the original components of the wheat grain. Genuine wholemeal flour has been stoneground.

Wholewheat Another deceptive term, as bleached white flour is wholewheat strictly speaking. This term is not used much in Australia; it does not necessarily mean wholemeal.

INDEX

Electricity and cooking, 48
Extraction, see *glossary*

Feedwell Café, 15
Fermentation, length of, 12
   minerals, 39
   see also *glossary*
Flour, aroma, 24
   bleaching, laws, 25
   extraction, 27
   maturity, 25, 74
   mixing, 30
   non wheat, 30
   organic, 24, 27,
     see also *glossary*
   roller milled, 26,
     see also *glossary*
   sifting, 28, 83
   stoneground, 27,
     see also *glossary*
   suitability for bread, 21-4
   temperature, 29
   varieties, 21
   water absorption, 24, 54, 81

Gas ovens, 48
Glazes, 66
Gluten, allergy, 20, 99
   assisting rising, 20
   in bread, 20, 54
   see also *glossary*
Gluten flour, 14
Gluten-free bread, 99
Grain sprouts, 44
Grinding wheat, 28

Hard flour, 20
Hard wheat, 19, see also *glossary*
Honey, 37-8
Hops leaven, 42

Imperial measures, 52

Kneading, 54, 74, 81, 83, see also
  glossary

Leaven bread, proving, 60
   technique, 59, 72
Leaven, consistency, 59
   contamination, 44

   failure, 25, 35, 44
   fruit, 41
   grain, 41
   maintenance, 43
   making, 40
   malt, 41
   miso, 42
   non wheat, 40
   rising, 48
   sour taste, 43
   wheat starch, 42
   see also *glossary*

Malt, dried, see *glossary*
     under Crystal malt
   leaven, 41
   liquid, 38, 82,
     see also *glossary*
Malted bran, 94
Maple syrup, 38
Maturity, see *glossary*
Meal, see *glossary*
Measurements, 52
Metric, 52
Millet, 87
Millet flour, 30
Minerals assimilation, 39
Miso leaven, 42, see also *glossary*
Molasses, 37-8
Monopoly mechanisation, 15
Muffins, 65, see also *glossary*

Neighbourhood bakery, 14
Nut meal, 36, 88
Nutrients, 10
Nutrition, 10

Oat flour, 30
Oats, 87, 89
Oil, 35, 58
Oil and yeast, 36
   substitutes, 36
   varieties and quality, 36, 51,
     see also *glossary* under
     Unrefined oil

Palm sugar, see *glossary*
Pastry flour, 19, see also *glossary*
Phytic acid, 10